'A highly comforting boo[k] [...] the pressures that we're a[ll under to achieve] – nevertheless gently reminds us that it is what we are, not what we do, that will always ultimately count.'
Alain de Botton, founder of The School of Life

'The paradox of success is real. The things that the system tells us will make us happy often don't. Perhaps it's time to stop trying to win and start working to contribute instead.'
Seth Godin, author of *The Song of Significance*

'This book changed how I think.'
Annie Macmanus, author of *The Mess We're In*

'A smart and insightful clarion call to everyone – my book of 2023.'
Farrah Storr, author of *The Discomfort Zone*

'A brilliant book, and so necessary. We have to get away from the idea that happiness is just over the next hill, and that everything will be better when we've achieved the next big thing. This is a crucial and joyful part of that conversation.'
Rebecca Seal, author of *Solo: How to Work Alone (and Not Lose Your Mind)*

'Such a powerful and thought-provoking read.'
Clover Stroud, author of *The Red of My Blood*

'I inhaled it in one sitting. It made my shoulders drop three inches by the time I'd read the first chapter. Why? It is a permission slip to escape "the achievement trap".'
Metro

The Success Myth

Letting Go of Having It All

Emma Gannon

PENGUIN BOOKS

TRANSWORLD PUBLISHERS
Penguin Random House, One Embassy Gardens,
8 Viaduct Gardens, London SW11 7BW
www.penguin.co.uk

Transworld is part of the Penguin Random House group of companies
whose addresses can be found at global.penguinrandomhouse.com

First published in Great Britain in 2023 by Torva
an imprint of Transworld Publishers
Penguin paperback edition published 2024

A CIP catalogue record for this book is available from the British Library.

ISBN
9781804990766

Typeset in Dante MT Pro by Jouve (UK), Milton Keynes.
Printed and bound in Great Britain by Clays Ltd, Elcograf S.p.A.

The authorized representative in the EEA is Penguin Random House Ireland,
Morrison Chambers, 32 Nassau Street, Dublin D02 YH68.

Penguin Random House is committed to a sustainable
future for our business, our readers and our planet. This book is made
from Forest Stewardship Council® certified paper.

For everyone,
no matter where you're at,
or where you're going

Contents

'Even if you achieve things that seem outwardly fabulous, an unhealed emotional injury will make you experience them as empty and unappealing. By contrast, recovering your emotional health will suffuse even small successes with joy, long before you achieve anything obviously spectacular.'

MARTHA BECK, *FINDING YOUR OWN NORTH STAR*

A Note

Before we begin, I am aware that we are living through heavy, scary, strange times. The cost of living is going up. The news is constant and seemingly always bad. Politics is a circus. Climate change is real. Social media is a minefield; we log on not knowing what will trigger us, or when. Record numbers of people are suffering from exhaustion and burnout. The Covid pandemic has left a whirlwind of mess in its wake. It's also true that, *on the whole*, it's a pretty good time to be alive. We have more now in this modern society than ever before. Evolving technology, which in turn opens up greater opportunity, growing literacy, quicker global transport, scientific breakthroughs and less extreme poverty. In so many ways, we are so lucky to be alive now, right now, on this planet.

The world is going through a vast amount of change in a very short period of time. It feels like turbulence on a plane.

I believe that before we tell ourselves that we're broken and need to change, we should consider whether it is actually the society we live in that is broken and needs to change. I also believe that by easing the demands we keep putting on *ourselves*, we can in tandem stop putting so much demand on the planet, on our natural resources. Yes, this book is about unpicking society's definitions of success and at the same time looking at what we truly want for ourselves, but it's also about the bigger picture. If we want to make change in a big way – it has to start with us going inwards. That doesn't mean putting the onus just on the individual to fix all the bigger systemic problems, but we can start somewhere. We can sit with ourselves; we can ask ourselves some big questions.

Let's take a collective breath for one moment. I'm going to tell you why I believe this book is needed and why it's actually more important than ever before to talk about the myths of 'success' (and how we are at risk of being conned along the way).

Introduction

Success Junkies

It was June 2018, and I'd been invited to give a keynote
speech about my latest book at a conference on the Isle of
Man. I was chauffeured to the airport in a silent black car
with spotless leather seats, and I was being paid more for this
one half-an-hour talk than I had earned for the entire previous month. I was wearing a new outfit and holding a new
handbag. I looked the part, and my life was panning out
exactly how I had imagined it. As I gazed out of the window
with the radio playing and London's buildings rolling past, I
felt *successful*. If I was going to have a 'girlboss' moment
(*sorry*), then this would be it: the moment all the self-help
business books had told me about. Entrepreneurial! Glamorous! Instagram followers! Agents, book deals, success! I
remember boarding the flight and finding my seat next to a

woman wearing pink lipstick and a beaded necklace. It was a short flight, and she was chatty, explaining to me that there was always a bumpy landing on to the island because of the sea winds and the dinky plane. We observed a woman in the seat in front of us ordering countless mini bottles of vodka while gripping on to the armrests, clearly prepping herself for a roller coaster ride. She obviously knew about the bumpy ride too.

'I always think it is going to be the end of my life on this flight,' the woman in front turned around to us to say, with terror in her voice.

'Well, I hope not!' I replied loudly, laughing nervously, looking out of the window at the wing. The plane was indeed small, and the wind was picking up.

The woman in lipstick next to me smiled. 'Well, if it does go down, I wouldn't mind too much. I've achieved everything I want to achieve,' she said peacefully, leaning back. 'I am content.'

Suddenly, I felt gripped by terror, like the woman with the mini vodkas. *I'm only just getting started,* I thought.

I have this keynote speech to deliver, for starters!

I have lots of things I need to SUCCEED at.

I am on a path to SUCCESS!

The captain spoke to us through the tannoy, sounding calm but laying down the facts, telling us to not leave our seats and keep our seat belts on. The turbulence was wild. Passengers were screaming. The woman beside me had warned me that the landing would be bumpy, but it *really* was. The plane touched down on what felt like just one wobbly wheel. The woman in front was now shaking, but the woman next to me was smiling. She really didn't seem afraid. Later that day, I thought about her, and what she meant by 'achieved everything she wanted to achieve'. She said she was 'content'. What did that even mean? Had she lost her marbles?

At that point, my entire identity revolved around my job. It was all that mattered, and all that I had. A few friends had casually pointed out to me that I was working a lot, and I would be very defensive. How dare they comment on my workload? How dare they pester me to come to the pub? I didn't have time for fun. I was on a mission. I would bat those comments away. If anyone even hinted that I was over-working, I would assume they were trying to distract me or 'didn't understand' my level of ambition. I *was* my achievements; I was a walking billboard of the 'things I was working on'. I was on the career ladder, and I wanted to be successful. I was competitive, driven, single-minded, and I had a lot to show for it on paper – and on social media.

Since the first day I entered the workplace, aged twenty-one, in a huge open-plan office with phones ringing and loud bosses and goals and praise, I had been seduced by the idea of success, ambition, growth and winning. I started thriving almost immediately, and I was intrigued by all the different people I was meeting with diverse opinions and backgrounds. This felt different to my identity at school, which was a place where I always felt behind, but in the working world I was zooming ahead. I started off at social media agencies, working for big shiny brands, then moved to Condé Nast, working for big shiny magazines. The fast-paced environment suited me, and I loved it. I wore heeled boots to the office. I worked late into the night during each office job in my twenties, with the offer of free pizza if you worked past nine p.m., which I loved because I preferred to be in the office than at home. I wanted to stay at work for as long as was possible. I didn't realize it at the time, but it was my own form of escapism. I felt safe inside the walls of the office. On Friday evenings, when my colleagues went home to their families for dinner, I would wander out into the street and think, *Now what?* It would take me a while to calm down physically from the adrenaline racing through my body from all the meetings and calls and dings and pings.

Moving to London was a big 'tick' on my list of dreams, and as my confidence grew, I felt like myself for the first time. Then I decided to go it alone, becoming self-employed, and a new success treadmill began. I had my own desk at home, and I'd work until it got dark, then I'd take my laptop to the sofa and work until the early hours, eating dinner there too. I might have been free from the corporate world, but as my own boss I was no better, I was still glued to the machine, to the industry, to the grind, to my own autopilot. If anything, I was even more hung up on success, as though I had something to prove. I wanted to show people they were wrong: those people who doubted I could ever make 'working for myself' a success.

However, after a few years of growing my business successfully, something was niggling at me inside. There was the first quiet whisper of something not being quite right. But I found I could shout loudly over it. This inner voice was nudging me, but it was being drowned out by talks, clapping audiences, Instagram likes and posting pictures of myself online. In reality, I felt like if someone prodded me hard enough, I would fall over, and everything would come crashing down around me. It was becoming harder and harder to ignore the feeling inside. There was one night in particular I knew something had to change.

Which brings us back to that evening on the Isle of Man. After I'd delivered my talk, taking off my Britney mic that had boomed throughout the huge auditorium, I went back to my hotel room and sat on the white sheets of the bed. I wasn't feeling relieved, or heightened, or joyful, or full of adrenaline. I felt completely flat. (If you google 'what is the opposite of "content"?' you get 'discontent'. My thesaurus gives me these synonyms: joyless, downcast, unpleased, dissatisfied.) I lowered my head into my hands, and I just sobbed. I looked around the room and felt incredibly . . . alone. I couldn't remember the last time I'd seen a friend, or remembered a birthday, or had done something for myself outside of work. People didn't ask how I was, because the assumption was that I was living the life I wanted. No one was checking in on me much, because why would they? My Instagram feed looked full, busy and exciting. I wore expensive suits, red lipstick and a big smile. Friends were messaging me saying 'you're killing it'. What was the 'it' I was killing? My soul, probably.

That night, I fell asleep to the voice of a friend who had sent me a long WhatsApp voice note in the middle of the night, detailing how she was doing, having just given birth, and updating me on what it was all like. She was tired, up late, her life had changed, going to the loo was a military operation, but she sounded good. I loved hearing from her and felt honoured to get the full story. She had just been through something life-changing. She was sleep-deprived. She was my friend. She still made time for me even though she was feeding a baby. And where had I been? Why was I not checking in with anyone? What exactly was this life that I was hell-bent on living?

I was lucky enough to enjoy what I did for a living for the most part and felt an inherent privilege that I could earn money as a 'knowledge worker', meaning I could set myself up independently as a 'digital nomad', working from anywhere as long as I had my laptop and Wi-Fi. I loved that my career was always there, like a buoyancy aid, something that I could lean on when I needed to, and it did make me happy sometimes. But I hadn't quite recognized the truth: that your job will never really love you back. Yes, it could support you financially, but it would never be there for you emotionally. It is not the comfort blanket you think it is. Even if you love something, if it takes over your life and starts to make you unwell, it is by definition an addiction of some sort. My obsession with outward success had gone so far that I would socialize mostly with acquaintances, rather than close friends, and only if I was feeling on form, hardly ever letting anyone see my vulnerable side. I always had to be working on something new. I felt as though I needed to be having a good day to be worthy of seeing people. I had become what digital-media consultant Jennifer Romolini calls 'an ambition monster'. Essentially, I was scared of being seen for who I really was. I wore a suit of success armour. I had to figure out how to get my life back. This is what this book is about.

What Is Success?

Many of us have access to lots of *things*: fast fashion, free online content, hundreds of cuisines on apps, next-day delivery, Black Friday sales, yet the statistics say quite clearly that we are not happy. Anxiety, burnout and depression rates are growing. The planet itself doesn't look too happy either, whether that's the rise in microplastics or climate change impacting our oceans and coastal ecosystems.

There is an irony at play here: as a society we are still craving the lofty heights of success like never before, yet our world does not look very 'successful' or 'happy' on paper. It doesn't seem to be working. The cultural rat race for success (however that looks to each of us) can often be never-ending: a distraction, a marketing technique, an obstacle course we didn't choose, a way to always be adding on more without taking a minute to breathe. A stick to beat ourselves with. We never feel like we're doing it right. How do we navigate our own definition of success when we see other people's successes play out on a loop every day via our phones?

This book is about getting to the root of what we actually

want from our own lives right now: not what looks good at a dinner party, not what gets you the most online validation, not what makes your parents proud, but figuring out what success looks like to *you* day to day. We are at a crucial turning point. It's time to ask ourselves what we want (not just materialistically) and work backwards to try and find it.

My hope in writing this book is not to try and convince you that reaching for the stars and following dreams isn't a good idea (it is – life is of course about moving forwards and having celebratory moments!) but to remind us all that society's expectations around big goals, milestones and trophies aren't always in line with the realities of what makes us feel individually satisfied. From my experience, the shiniest bits we see online, hear about, or see in the news are hardly ever the shiniest bits behind the scenes. Instagram has been said to be other people's 'highlight reels'– and the very concept of 'success' marketing in society is the collective highlight reel that sucks us in. How would you like your life to look, if you didn't have to advertise it to others?

Everywhere I go, people around me are uprooting their lives. Record numbers of people have left their jobs since the beginning of the pandemic. Are we finally waking up to the fact that so much of life happens in the cracks between the chasing of success: that money, fame and endless materialism won't save us, that they won't be the answer to our problems? Are we noticing that the 'gurus' and idols and high achievers who sell the key to success actually don't possess the formula for our own individual happiness?

The Missing Link

For the past six years, I've been conducting a weekly interview on my podcast, *Ctrl Alt Delete*, with someone who has 'succeeded' in their (usually creative) field. It's a careers podcast without the corporate bullshit, and I get to gently interrogate my guest about how on earth they've climbed their own ladder and designed their own lives, and pick up any additional pointers on how they've stayed sane. It's been hugely enjoyable, not only to probe these interviewees with personal questions but also to meet them in person, which means I have heard memorable stories both on and off the mic. I have now interviewed over four hundred outwardly successful people, including activists who have changed laws, politicians making big decisions, Oscar-winning scriptwriters, sports stars, famous writers, experts in their field of niche research, philosophers, psychologists, spiritual teachers, actors, doctors, singers; you name it. There are a variety of stories, including people who have come from nothing, people who have come from huge privilege, people who have won awards, been bereaved, walked the red carpet, lost everything, gained everything, started again, reached millions, had panic attacks, spoken on huge stages, and held the world's attention and had its adoration. Without realizing it, I've become an accidental expert in interviewing and analyzing people on their outward 'success' while also being privy to their internal thoughts 'behind the scenes', and all the flaws and imperfections that come with being human. I've noticed that some people would confidently share their achievements, while others would shy away from them; some interviewees would exaggerate their achievements, while a few wouldn't even seem to care about them. Some people took complete responsibility for their success, putting it down to hard work only, while others put it down to luck; some owned their talent, some had major impostor syndrome, some put it down to God, and some accepted that it was a mixture of many things. Many attributed their success to the love and support of their parents, teachers or just one person who believed in them. It's been fascinating to find patterns and common threads to pull on.

I started the podcast because I wanted to know the secrets to success. I wanted to peek behind the curtain and figure out what makes someone successful at what they do. Are all these people, with their glowing Wikipedia pages, financial security and full award cabinets, happier and more fulfilled than everyone else? Do they feel as though they've ascended to another level of life?

I quickly realized that most of the time, in short, the answer is no. No matter how high up the ladder of society's definition of success people climb, I've seen the same insecurities, doubts, health problems, domestic stress, creative block and uncertainty over the future. I've seen people reach their life's goal and realize that instead of a marching band celebrating the long-awaited milestone, they just want to crawl into bed in a dark room for a week. I've had people admit that when they finally reached their dreams, it was then that their life started to fall apart. I've heard stories of people who look like they're 'smashing it' but are actually having an internal crisis. I've heard stories of how influxes of money can tear relationships apart, and about how money makes you paranoid. And now I feel compelled to open up the conversation. Is being outwardly successful everything it's cracked up to be? Is the 'Great Resignation' (a term coined by Professor Anthony Klotz, describing the record number of people quitting their jobs since the beginning of the Covid-19 pandemic) happening because we are all finally exhausted from the endless, relentless hustle?

On and off the mic, there is one thing most of my guests had in common: a surprising sense of *I've done all this stuff and I still don't feel like I'm enough.* When I was growing up, I felt successful people had an air about them that suggested they'd solved life's riddle, that they had cracked the code! And yet, once I'd met them in person, it didn't really feel that way at all. I was deflated by this: there is a reason a rags-to-riches story sells. We want to hear that it's possible to change our whole life in three simple steps and live happily ever after. We like happy endings. They are neat; they are easier to understand.

So many of us were taught to keep climbing up the ladder (school, university, work, promotions, family, home, success), so we believe that, surely, there is an end point, a moment where you feel like *you've made it*. This is what I was wanting from these interviews: for people to say that there is a moment of relief at a 'finish line', a comforting assurance that one day we will find the treasure at the end of the rainbow and live happily ever after. But not once did I ever get the sense that there is that golden, everlasting moment. In fact, on the other side of the 'success' coin, there was something much darker lurking. A loss of self. A loss of relationships, or relationships that became purely transactional. A loss of trust. Mental health problems. Boundaries being overstepped. A skewed sense of self-worth. Online threats and trolling. Falling into the trap of prioritizing the opinions of strangers. Situations that would retrigger macro- or microtrauma. An existential crisis. I was astounded by just how many 'successful' people whispered to me, *'None of this impressive stuff has made my inner problems go away.'* We still struggle to believe this because success is so seductive. Of course, we could list many worse or different positions to be in, but this topic of society's obsession with success is still worthy of analyzing and unpicking. Everything is relative, and with context and sensitivity all our modern issues are worth discussing. I can't help but be curious about this. Why not question why so many 'successful' people suffer too? There seems to be a missing link.

A Wake-up Call

Peeking behind the curtain of so many of these people's lives and careers led me to feel even more curious about the wider subject of success. It inspired me to look into my own definition of success, my own gremlins, my own narratives, my own preconceptions. Does my ego believe I should be more successful? Am I chasing success for a particular reason? Has my life changed since achieving some of my shiny exterior goals? How ambitious am I actually? How often does our definition of success change? These were questions I was asking myself pre-pandemic, and then when the world shut down for months at a time, many of us were forced to look at our lives in closer detail. We asked ourselves some big questions while our plans were put on pause. Do we even like our jobs? Do we even like ourselves? What does success mean when we're all stuck at home, alone? What does collective success look like? These are the juicy questions I'll be diving into throughout this book's chapters on happiness, money, work and beyond.

Before the lockdowns of 2020 and 2021, I was busy. Looking back, I wasn't necessarily happy, but I was distracted. My life looked good on the outside, and I had no reason to open a can of worms. But once lockdown hit, I realized something felt off. Yes, it was a pandemic, so I was not leaving the house much, but I was staying in most nights (even when the lockdown rules eased up), numbing out with wine, shying away from any interesting opportunities, and I blamed my withdrawal on being 'introverted'. I kept social contact to a minimum and I just stayed in my cocoon, not wanting to come out. I was a caterpillar and had no clue why I wasn't interested in finding ways to emerge and spread my wings. Change was occurring externally, but massive change was also starting to happen inside.

The pandemic was awful in so many ways, truly terrible – *and* for many of us it was also a chance to look closely at our lives. It was a pause that we wouldn't have had otherwise.

For me, it really was a jolt of realization. I was lucky; I had no real personal dramas, no major illness, I was simply offered the opportunity to slow down and spend a lot of time reflecting on my life. I was able to realize how much I was drifting, lost, retreating inwards. I wanted to rip everything up, cancel my old definition of success, interrogate everything, start again, work out what my boundaries were and who my core friends were. I was starting to slowly realize that the maths wasn't adding up, but I was still very afraid to confess it externally. I felt guilty. *What do you mean all your dreams came true and you're still not happy?* My inner critic was bleating things like: *What on earth is wrong with you? You know other people have it much worse? You should be happy.* But that's not how happiness works. You can't demand it, or force it, or magic it into existence. It was time to change my prepandemic idea of success. I had to kill off that former version of myself, which meant leaning into change and grieving my past life. It felt scary, uncomfortable and painful to say goodbye to an identity that no longer served me.

Not knowing where to turn, I got in touch with a life coach. 'I think I'm a workaholic,' I said to her. She quizzed me lightly. Does my self-worth come from output? Is my identity tied to work? Do I feel guilty for resting? Am I hard on myself? Do I crack the work whip even when I am in need of a holiday? Does work come first, before anything else? I answered yes to pretty much everything. But surely workaholics are men in suits who don't want to see their families, who hide away in their sad office buildings and have affairs with receptionists? Whereas I'm a writer and creator who mostly works from home. How could I fit that stereotype? In the worst of it, I remember listening to a podcast with a self-proclaimed workaholic New York art critic who said he only likes to socialize with people who he can talk about work with, as he finds all other conversation unstimulating and boring. I remember nodding along in agreement. Crikey.

This book blends my personal experience with the findings from my most fascinating interviews. I am a recovering success addict. Past descriptions of my former self feel totally alien to me now. Having come out the other side of a definite obsession around maintaining success and achievement (with the help of talking therapy, life coaching, friends and family), I've been able to pinpoint why I felt like I could wrap a cloak of success around myself in order to try and mask some other deeper problems and avoid dealing with them. I've also been able to see why I never quite felt like I had 'arrived', despite achieving my wildest dreams. I have realized that desperate need for success is often covering up some deeper stuff that is worth exploring with loved ones, through different kinds of therapy or even by writing a journal (to start with). There can be an inherent feeling of guilt attached to not feeling grateful for what we have. Guilt can really eat away at us. I hope by opening up the conversation in this book, we can shed the guilt, start to feel less alone in our emotions, and feel lighter, no matter where we are at.

A Raised Eyebrow

Perhaps you also already have some preconceptions about this topic: *What is there really to say about success? Come on, stop moaning, can't you just enjoy it? Surely the more successful you are, the happier you are? What's wrong with spending your whole life chasing traditional success?* Or even, *Don't we need an idea of success to give us hope?* Before I picked up my pen to write this book, these points gave me pause, and I've kept them in mind as I've written each chapter. But I've realized that when we perpetuate stereotypes about success (i.e. that person has XYZ so they're set for life, end of) we are missing so much nuance – and nuance is a very crucial and forgotten element of this conversation.

Of course, in many ways, success enables us to become more comfortable: financially, materially and physically. But being *more comfortable* is different to being *happier*. Starting from a place of comfort, I want to acknowledge that unpicking and analyzing the topic of success is a huge privilege in itself. I have the time and space to sit around pondering it, writing this book on it, talking at length with my interviewees, which isn't possible when you're existing in survival mode. I understand this and see this. This is not my outlet to moan about the downsides of success, like an out-of-touch celebrity not realizing their mic is on; instead it's an intimate look at why we are so seduced by it, and a place to offer some advice on how we can break free from the things that end up trapping us. A place to look at it objectively as a thing being sold to us on every corner. If anything, it's the book that I would like to have read all those years ago, when the bookshelves were only full of perfect women with perfect lives, because hearing the subtleties and conflicting emotions of other people's experiences may have helped me go a little easier on myself. It might have saved me from a few sleepless nights and two a.m. crises thinking about how I was doing everything wrong and everyone else was doing it right. It might help a few more people learn to reframe their definition of success, *enjoy* achieving their goals and also enjoy getting there. It might have stopped me from having a burnout breakdown through overwork.

We start to receive cultural messages from early childhood on what success looks like: praise, rewards, climbing, claps.

I've seen some five-year-olds even have a 'graduation ceremony' from nursery, wearing a miniature mortar board, being praised for their achievements. These moments are positive, of course, but they also start us off on the bottom rung of the success ladder, one that we continue chasing in other ways for our entire adulthood. We are told to strive and strive in an upwards motion, but we are not equipped to deal with the realities of our day-to-day lives. We keep hitting various milestones and feel deflated. Oftentimes, dreams don't tend to match up with reality. When we finally figure out that our drive for 'success' isn't making us feel good in the long run, the question we start to ask is: are we even chasing after the right thing?

Success changes from culture to culture, but on the whole, when I asked podcast interviewees, friends and strangers a series of questions about success for this book, including 'What did you think success meant, when you were growing up?', the answers that came back were along the same lines:

- Obtaining material things.
- Getting a degree.
- Buying a house.
- Getting a good job.
- Finding a life partner/getting married.
- Having kids.

Towards the end of the book (don't jump ahead!), I include a list of the things that my interviewees say feel like success now, after having either achieved these milestones, tweaked their goals or ditched them completely, shapeshifting them into other aspirations that feel more aligned with their personal definition of happiness. Of course, we need things to strive for, but throughout this book I am looking into the idea of success in more depth: explaining how a blinkered approach to striving distracts us from other meaningful moments, but also exploring whether there's a way to strive and feel fulfilled along the way. Is there a happy medium? I believe the reason so many of us – hard-workers, strivers, self-proclaimed ambitious people, parents, creatives, citizens, activists, or just-getting-through-the-day people – all feel confused and lack a sense of satisfaction is because we've been lied to. We are chasing the scam of outward traditional success (thinking there is always 'more') where our ego gets a boost and we acquire some things but it doesn't actually end up impacting our inner landscape in a positive or lasting way. Instead, we should be given the tools to unlock what our own preferred version of life is and find ways to move towards that. We are all on different paths, yet we are all taught to want the same things. We are made to feel slightly mad if we turn down opportunities that we are 'supposed' to want.

There is a quote attributed to Picasso that claims, 'Every child is an artist. The problem is how to remain an artist once he grows up.' I think about this a lot: outside of art, in life in general, we move further and further away from who we really are. As children we already have our gifts, then we grow up to discover them, and then society around us moves us further and further away from them. We are still only offered up around ten 'main' jobs to peruse in a careers leaflet, with traditional training schemes schooling us to be another cog in the machine. It starts with school, but we don't quite realize the treadmill we've been on until we reach a 'mid-life crisis'. When we reach a certain stage in life, most of us start to question everything we've ever been told: the great *unlearning. What key things weren't we taught at school? What are our parents wrong about? Why are we socialized to go along with things we don't like or want? Do we really have to spend our working lives sitting in cubicles under strip lighting? Is marriage needed? Do we have to have kids? Why weren't we taught more information about mental health? How do we find our own path back to ourselves?*

This book will question the classic tickboxes we are constantly sold. Many of us are on the treadmill without questioning it. Chasing a shiny and impressive LinkedIn page more than a life you actually like. Trying to impress other people more than sitting comfortably with yourself.

Maxing out credit cards on things that will look good to the outside world, but stress you out at night. Going to a party with people you don't even like. Adding on things to an already unmanageable life. This isn't about quitting everything, or never striving for more: quite the opposite. It's about striving and caring and investing in your life more than ever before – but in a way *you* want, in a direction only you know is right for you. Whether your life goals consist of sitting on the sofa with a cup of tea at the end of the day with no drama, or climbing Kilimanjaro, or writing a poetry book, or pruning a small garden, or performing a life-saving operation, or having Tuesdays off. This book will help you reach your goals intentionally, rather than getting swept away with the crowd.

Use this book as a compass, not a map. For so long, I'd replaced my inner wisdom with the wisdom sold to me in books, listicles and podcasts. Repeat after me: other people do not have the answer. I encourage you to use your own inner wisdom as you read this book. Read it slowly, question it, take things with a pinch of salt if they don't work for you – this book exists to prompt you to re-examine *your* relationship with success. You will not find 'all the answers' in this book, because no one book can do that, but it will prompt you to think about success in new ways. You already have the answers to your life's big questions. We might not know exactly where we're going, but we can point ourselves in the direction that feels most right. We are the experts on our own lives, but with so much noise around us, it can be easy to forget that.

It's strange really, to embark on writing a book about success, when my definition of success has changed so much since I wrote my first book seven years ago. What I want to achieve here looks different to all my other books. A big part of me wanted SUCCESS in bright city-neon lights. But now I'm going into the process differently. I used to think success could be measured by always seeing my book in a shop window (a rare occurrence, sadly), or drinking champagne at a shiny launch party (Covid derailed that dream for a while), or being on a bestseller list (which happened once, and I celebrated by going to a family member's house for a barbecue. It rained and we burnt the sausages). Real life doesn't stop once you reach a career high, but we expect to be on cloud nine for ever because that is what we're taught to believe. When we're not on cloud nine, we feel like we've failed, that we've done something wrong; we must have not revised hard enough for the test. But I'm going to show that's not true. The narrative of cloud nine success is a trap.

I'm writing this with absolutely no idea how it will go down and, compared with my previous books, much less attachment to the outcome. I am sat here, at ten past eight on a Tuesday morning, writing while the birds chirp away in the background. A far cry from my old chaotic ways, I'm drinking some water with a hydration tablet in it, I'm looking out at the trees in my garden blowing gently in the wind, with slightly grey clouds looming above. I will have lunch, do some other work to pay my bills, maybe watch a film and get an early night. The hustle has quietened. Whether this book becomes a huge bestselling success or ends up in someone's bin, I know my life will more or less stay exactly the same afterwards. But I will have really enjoyed the process and it will have meant something. I've changed my own life for the better through writing it. I've tasted some tiny snippets of those dizzying heights of success, and what goes up has to come down again. I know that if you had issues before success, those same issues will be there, if not exacerbated by the new complications piled on top. The life I'm living at this very moment is the bit that I now appreciate. The first mug of hot tea in the morning, an hour of a good TV show, long walks on crisp autumnal days wearing a soft scarf, a pub roast and laughter, family coming to stay, the parakeets that fly over my house, the funny text from a best friend, turning the pages of a good novel: these things bring me the most joy, not a round of applause on stage or getting a thousand Instagram likes. But it's not really important what success is to me; this is about you figuring out what it means to you – this book will help you do it on your own terms.

Since changing my relationship with success, I have found myself attracting amazing people back into my life and attracting better energy in all areas. Likewise, I have lost friends who are no longer on my wavelength as they make their own way on a different success journey. I have connected more deeply with my loved ones. I set myself achievable goals, and I'm no longer interested in acquiring loads of expensive 'stuff'. As a result, I have never been healthier, and day to day I don't feel overly stressed. As spiritual teacher Bryon Katie says: 'We only do three things in life: we sit, we stand, we lie horizontal. The rest is just a story.' I would also add that everything (beyond survival and basic needs) is just stuff. It's how we feel and what we do amongst the stuff that matters.

Beyond my personal epiphany, I can see our definition of success is changing: from the decline of traditional celebrity culture and our rejection of the drive for productivity at the expense of wellbeing, to a collective realization that there is no destination and we are more than our job, more than the things we produce. We are finally ready for a shift, and to say 'no' to the treadmill of traditional success and Keeping Up with the Joneses (or Kardashians) at all times.

Even with the best support, it's really hard to figure out

what we want our lives to look like day to day. It's even harder when we feel on our own. Have you ticked things off but still feel like something is missing? Do you feel like your current tick list is a bit of a scam? Does true satisfaction feel as though it's never quite within reach? Do you feel like you've had a taste of success but it doesn't quite feel right – or you don't feel you have the right tools to actually *enjoy* it while it's happening? You've got the right book in your hands. I hope you find that reading it gives you more ways to think about what you want from your life and reveals the fact that the answer to happiness and success is not as clear-cut as we are made to believe.

Those are all my questions, so let's now dig into some of the answers. I hope that by the end of the book, you realize what a success you are, in whatever way you decide to define it. It's time to get back in the driving seat of our own lives.

Emma Gannon
London, 2023

ONE

There Is No Success 'Formula'

'Do you know the *Ultimate Success Formula?*
Learn the four step process and start
taking massive action in your life!'

TONY ROBBINS, 29 AUGUST 2016

I'm allergic to gurus telling us about the easy steps to success.
Following the publication of my second book, *The Multi-Hyphen Method*, I was invited into many different public and
private spaces (including charities, schools, offices and even
Amazon HQ) with the brief to 'come and tell people how
to be successful in what they do'. Success in the traditional
sense: more money, more visibility, more everything. This
wasn't the aim of the book. The book was about being a
multi-hyphenate, and working in a different, multi-faceted

way. Telling other people 'how' to be successful was not my agenda, but I was quickly put in the self-help-author box. People start to treat you as though you have the four-digit code to a safe, and if you tell others the digits, then they too will be able to access the pathway to success. It was like asking me to come in and tell everyone which haircut to get. *I don't know what you want, I don't know your history, I don't know you.* I didn't have the answer to 'the success equation', I just wanted to help people see a way to do things differently. I didn't *know* why things had gone particularly well that year. It was probably a combination of things, but I felt uncomfortable with the role of 'advice giver' or 'motivational speaker' and refused to do it. At Q&As, if someone asked me what they should do to succeed, I turned the questions back on to them instead. If someone acts like they have the answers to what you should do with your life, be wary of them. Everyone is the sole custodian of their own life, and blanket 'formulas' miss out a key point: the world isn't set up to allow everyone to thrive equally. Big-time self-help gurus may act like they have *the* universal winning formula, but they don't.

Anyone Can Make It!

The 'American Dream' was a phrase I understood from a very young age. Ah, the seductive idea that anyone, if they just worked hard enough, could achieve whatever they wanted to! But in our culture of 'success marketing', the idea that 'one day' life will fall into place for evermore, if we just do the right things in the right order, is one of the biggest cons sold to us. With adverts and media all around us promoting everything we need to 'win' at life, it's no wonder we are obsessed with cracking the formula to success. It seems so simple, if only we knew the equation. One of the reasons 'success' is such an emotionally fraught topic is because we all know it's unfair. For every Lady Gaga, David Beckham or Will Smith, there are arguably other singers/ footballers/actors who are equally as talented, but for various reasons never make it to worldwide superstardom. For every Oprah success story, there is racial inequality still permeating the culture at a production company. For every young working-class footballer, there are thousands of youngsters with the exact same CV who never make any team. There are seven billion of us, we absolutely need equality of opportunity, but if we are *all* striving to be *the* next superstar, by default many of us are going to be disappointed. This is the problem: we see a small number of people are at the top and this is sold to us as the 'best' way to live a life. A narrative of public life and living with excess is constantly showcased as being 'The Dream' until we look more closely. The idea that everyone can 'have it all' keeps us on the treadmill: keeps us working late, keeps us spending and keeps making other people money.

We could forensically pick apart the reasons why one person succeeds when another doesn't, but there would be no one answer, as there are so many variables. Hard work, natural talent, privilege and luck are just a few of the elements that play a part, but we often overlook the full picture, as very few people publicly acknowledge everything that contributed to their success.

There are so many factors involved in why something happens, or doesn't happen; society is still systemically unequal and unfair, and many things are often out of our control. That's not to say it won't happen. It *might*. It *could*. And we might feel like we should do everything in our power to try, if that's what we want. For example, I would like one of my novels to be turned into a TV show. It feels like a wild dream, something that I could spend the next ten years doggedly focused on, but the reality is that my dream coming true has nothing to do with me any more. I've done my bit, in terms of putting it into the world. I wrote the novel. It exists. It's available. Ultimately, it's to do with a stranger somewhere, sat in another building, deciding if they want to take it on, and then all the other factors lining up: talent, timing, money, luck, right place, right time, whether it's good enough. If it happened, at this point it would actually have had little to do with me. I could increase my chances of making my dream come true by writing letters, emailing my agent constantly, spending every single weekend trying to meet people and network, sending countless emails, looking up names on industry databases and putting my name forward for endless opportunities, but none of that is a guarantee of anything happening at all. We hear stories of people sitting in Starbucks and getting a career-defining call seemingly out of the blue. 'Hard work' does not always equal the end result you are after, but it's also worth mentioning that without it, you remain even further away.

We can spend our entire lives trying to work out other people's success formula – or we can try a new formula, our own formula – which is doing our very best with what we have and finding ways to enjoy ourselves along the way. We can't copy and paste someone else's success story. This is a pervasive myth, which drives a whole industry of 'career success' courses and books: 'I did it – so you can too!'

So, how do you go about discovering your *own* formula?

'Having It All' Is Bullshit

We've all heard the phrase coined by Helen Gurley Brown in her 1986 book of the same name. The blurb on the back cover of *Having It All* reads, 'The editor of *Cosmopolitan* gives advice on dealing with men and women, sex, marriage, career success, becoming more attractive, making money, and staying healthy.' And many of us are still trying to master this impossible formula of juggling everything. For us, there is a never-ending list of things to achieve. There is a pressure on both men and women: the pressure of having to be many things at once. (It's worth mentioning Gurley Brown didn't even like the phrase 'Having It All', but her publishers did.)

Today's generation of women are trying to shake off these 'shoulds' like a wet dog after a swim, but there's no doubt we're *still* plagued by the concept of having it all. It follows us around. The pressure to 'do modern life well' is becoming a larger, more complicated maze, and many of us don't feel satisfied because the options are endless and other people's success is often shoved in our faces. Are you being a good parent, boss, daughter, friend? Are you achieving this elusive work-life balance? Are you doing it all perfectly? Are you managing to do it all, with dwindling resources and expensive childcare and inequality? Elizabeth Gilbert, a passionate advocate for creativity and freedom, and author of multiple books, including *Eat Pray Love*, says: 'I felt the need to speak out once more against the subtle tyranny of the word BALANCE, which haunts and punishes modern women more and more every day. We are constantly being told that we should be achieving balance – that we should somehow exquisitely be negotiating the relationships between our work lives, our home lives, our romantic lives, our health and well-being, our spiritual selves. You can't read an interview with a famous woman these days that the journalist does not applaud her for having achieved BALANCE . . . and then if you turn the pages of that magazine, you will find ten more articles showing how you can achieve balance too. Be careful. The word BALANCE has tilted dangerously close, I fear, to the word PERFECT – another word that women use as weapons against themselves and each other.' I am wary of chasing balance, and instead go in and out of spending time on different things (projects, social time, holidays, intense deadlines), rather than feeling like I have to win at doing absolutely everything in a perfect, balanced way. Sometimes, life is unbalanced, and that's OK.

The popular retort from a lot of people I interview is that you can have it all, *but just not all at the same time.* This always made me scratch my head, because it shows that at any one point in your life, you have to sacrifice something, which is the definition of *not* being able to have it all. Why not say it as it is? We simply cannot have it all in just one life. We cannot be in two places at once. We cannot be cloned. Admit it. From an early age, I've made peace with knowing I won't be having it 'all'. I've realized that sacrifices may need to be made in order to live the life I want. I've always known I probably don't want to have children, for example, and that's not because I am a career maniac who only cares about smashing my goals and earning money (at least not any more). Life is finite, so every time we make a decision, something else has to give. By doing one thing, we are by definition letting go of another. By choosing one thing, you are ultimately not choosing something else. And there are many situations in which we cannot choose, because circumstances and logistics have already made the decision for us.

Living in tune with the reality of our finite lives is more freeing than trying to be everything to everyone all the time. But there still seems to be a pervasive sense of inner shame that comes with the inability to juggle it all, especially from women. We can start to uncover why such shame and guilt live so strongly within us and show ourselves compassion. We simply can't dance backwards in high heels any longer, or, at least, we don't want to.

The Path to Traditional 'Success' Is Gendered

Men completely dominate the *Sunday Times* list of the richest two-hundred and fifty people in Britain every year, with women usually only appearing if they have family or marriage connections, rather than earning a place on it in their own right. This massive discrepancy is down to what a lot of people call the 'glass ceiling'. It's deflating that this is still a huge modern-day issue, with women and mothers often put on the back burner and left to figure things out themselves with hardly any support. On the *Economist*'s 2022 glass-ceiling index, the US fell down the list to the twentieth spot, for providing no federally mandated parental leave. The UK sat at number seventeen. The top four countries for working women were Sweden, Iceland, Finland and Norway.

An example of this ongoing issue: In 2021, Terri White left her editor-in-chief role at *Empire* magazine because it just wasn't set up in a way for her to thrive as a working mother. It was shocking and eye-opening for Terri to admit something that seems (naively on my part) 'of the past': that a woman with a job and a child might be forced to pick one or the other. She says, in a *New Statesman* piece: 'For the first six months of my son's life I stayed at home. For the next year I went back to work as the editor-in-chief of a magazine. It was a job I loved; it coloured in the bits of me that my son couldn't, nor should have to. But the inflexibility and unsustainable hours proved impossible. And when I eventually chose to leave, it wasn't the rent I worried about finding, it was the childcare fees.'

And it's not just the inflexibility of our workplaces that is pushing women out. There is an imbalance inherent in our culture. Masculine 'power' is rewarded, and we see it everywhere: from the storylines in modern movies to the fairytales we read our kids at night, from tales of slaying dragons to the Bible, from Greek myths to the way historical events have been recorded. The retelling over and over again of these narratives has set in stone what 'success' and 'triumph' are expected to look like, which values and characteristics will win out, and, crucially, what power looks like, and *who* gets to be successful. According to *Harvard Business Review*, 'Compared to men, women listed more goals, and a smaller proportion of women's goals were related to achieving power. These findings dovetailed with the results of prior research that, relative to women, men are more motivated by traditional ideas of power (being in control, decision-making, status). These differences contribute to men holding higher leadership positions than women.' We conflate success with power because it is the dominant narrative in our culture.

I asked Elizabeth Lesser, author of *Cassandra Speaks: When Women Are the Storytellers, the Human Story Changes*, about these gendered narratives when it comes power and success. Why is masculine 'power' (alpha leadership, assertiveness, competitiveness) celebrated so much in society when more generalized female attributes (motherhood, community, softer traits) are overlooked? She said: 'The stories steer men toward what is coded masculine: stoicism, warriorship and violence. I look to history to explain why there's a lack of celebration of women's versions of success. In every era of history and every corner of the globe – from ancient China, Japan, Greece and Rome, from modern history, and from the adventure stories and leadership texts – power and success are linked with domination and aggression; leadership is linked with the warrior code, and women's voices and concerns are largely non-existent. What if women's emotional intelligence, relational natures, roles as nurturers, healers, mothers and teachers had been respected, sought after and woven into the story of power and success?' I love this question: what if success could look different and be seen through an alternative lens?

There are some biological differences, with studies showing that female mammals respond to stress in a different way to males. Shelley Taylor, a researcher at UCLA, coined the term 'tend and befriend' and explains how female mammals are more likely to react in a nurturing way to stress, rather than the more masculine impulse of fight-or-flight. 'Tend' refers to protecting offspring and keeping vulnerable ones safe, and 'befriend' to seeking out their social group or community for collective defence. Anecdotally, this appears to be reflected across corporate America, where many female leaders I have personally worked with deal with stress often by trying to create a sense of union and belonging in the workplace and in their teams, rather than just barking orders or telling everyone what to do from a position of power. Tend-and-befriend is extremely powerful, and achieves impactful results, just in a different way than we're used to. It's more about sharing and nurturing ideas and bringing people together. Of course, this research generalizes data into two binaries and there is nuance when it comes to gender across a spectrum, but it's important to show 'success' and successful outcomes in many different ways. There is not just one way to feel powerful in your life, and you do not need to be confined to a box.

It's important to state the facts about probability for success too, and how it is skewed in favour of the deeper grooves that have already been carved out by male-centric history books. We can't have it all, especially when we haven't even got equal amounts of the pie. But what we can do is work with what we've got and be aware of the truth of our reality. It's not that women aren't powerful, it's that masculine traits of having power 'over' someone else are currently rewarded in the workplace and in politics. Our collective goal should be for everyone to thrive in their own way. As Elizabeth Lesser says, to change things, 'men in this century are going to have to want to change as much as women wanted to change'. The key to achieving this is that it isn't seen as a duty or a chore, or as 'giving up' anything, but instead embracing the fact that a more inclusive approach is beneficial to all of us now and will also bring positive change to future generations.

I asked Lesser about whether a more equal version of success for men and women is possible post-pandemic or in the near future. Even though she is clear on the obstacles, she sounded optimistic. 'The pandemic was an accelerator of this change and women and men have to make sure it stays that way. I dream of men fearlessly reclaiming words and traits that have been coded feminine: feelings, empathy, communication. I dream of women reclaiming traits that have been coded masculine: ambition, confidence, authority. But what I dream of most is women and men mixing it up and blending it all together.' Blending it all together means ripping up the old way and making room for a brand new one. It means 'success' may look different to each household, each couple, each family unit, instead of us trying to force ourselves into a one-size-fits-all model.

Privilege and Success

Just as I know that my experiences as a young woman in the workplace in the noughties may have kept me feeling frustrated and held back in some ways, it's also important to acknowledge where I've had a leg-up in other ways. When I was in my early twenties, someone tweeted me to 'check my privilege'. At first, I didn't really know what it meant. I associated aristocratic levels of poshness with being privileged, and so my first instinct was to feel slightly defensive. I didn't go to boarding school. I don't know any earls. I don't sound like Joanna Lumley in the 2008 Privilege car insurance ad. I thought I had a normal-ish upbringing, I had a laborious summer job when I was a teenager; growing up, I didn't know any writers or famous people! I know, I know. *Oh dear, Emma. You had a lot to learn.*

I was in the depths of hardworkitis (a word I may have just made up), where you believe that you have worked hard for everything you have and it is just you and your 'work ethic' that got you there. It's a condition in which you feel like you got absolutely everything because of your own tenacity and gifts to the world. (The experts call it 'self-enhancing bias'.) In fact, of course, the privileges I had, and still have, are endless. I always knew I would have a roof over my head if the shit hit the fan. I had a family who could financially support me during university. I was surrounded by love and praise growing up. I am able-bodied, English-speaking and white, living in a democratic Western country with an abundance of opportunity. Nothing is perfect, but my head start in life was significant. This doesn't take away from any of my hard work, it's just admitting that my efforts were more likely to get me somewhere. Society's inbuilt prejudices gave me a solid foundation to benefit from. It's important to acknowledge these things when talking about success.

The current system is not set up to provide everyone with an equal starting point. Some people are fortunate enough to be able to reach their goals more easily than others, be it via their gender or race, or through nepotism, contacts, or financial advantage. I once knew someone who wanted to start a travel blog, so in order to create the content she needed, she self-funded a luxurious round-the-world trip to different beautiful beaches, taking a very expensive camera with her. This headstart for that particular niche career would be out of reach for many people; it would have simply been impossible or nearly impossible to create the necessary foundations for that specific outlet. Countless founders launch their businesses by raising money via a 'friends and family round', which puts them in better stead than those starting from scratch. Interns in many big companies often get let in through the side-door through family friends with connections. You go on to Wikipedia, intrigued about a new actor in a TV show, and you see that their parents own the production company.

So, despite being plastered across coffee mugs and T-shirts, phrases like 'We all have the same twenty-four hours as Beyoncé' are misleading. As many people have pointed out over the years, although we do technically have the same number of hours on earth each day as Beyoncé, crucially, we (probably) don't have the same talents as Beyoncé, we don't have the same lifestyle as Beyoncé, and we don't have the same entourage as Beyoncé. Just because we all have the same hours, it doesn't mean we can achieve the same things. It's a ridiculous way to pep talk someone and it's strange how popular this quote has become.

The Myth of (Just) Hard Work

In December 2021, Molly-Mae Hague, the former *Love Island* star and creative director of fashion brand Pretty Little Thing, made an appearance on *The Diary of a CEO* podcast, hosted by *Dragon's Den* star Steven Bartlett. She was being quizzed about her career to date, her work ethic, her business moves, and the story of how, at just twenty-two, she had made millions and attracted millions of young people to follow her every move on Instagram. She declared that she believes we are all capable of doing whatever we want with our lives. On paper, her idea that we can all attempt to be anything we want to be is motivating: 'I understand we all have different backgrounds and we're all raised in different ways and we do have different financial situations, but if you want something enough you can achieve it.' I also used to believe that hard work alone enables anyone to achieve their dreams, and I understand why she said it, but it misses out a huge part of the conversation. The elephant in the room is that there are so many other factors at play. Simply 'wanting' something enough suggests that equal amounts of hard work results in equal amounts of success. It suggests that people who haven't got the life they want don't work as hard. When we say, 'If you want something enough you can achieve it,' it suggests that there is a formula that simply needs to be applied (x hours equals x result), but it's just not the case.

A friend admitted that her shifts working at a city-centre coffee shop years ago were *much* harder graft than writing her recent book. 'Hard work' looks different to each of us.

Kim Kardashian recently came under fire for saying in *Variety* magazine: 'I have the best advice for women in business. Get your fucking ass up and work. It seems like nobody wants to work these days.' In my opinion, it's not that people aren't working hard, it's that they aren't being rewarded properly. It may be true that people like Molly-Mae and the Kardashians are gifted at the entrepreneurial side of things, but this doesn't automatically mean they have worked *harder*. It doesn't have to be a bad thing, or an icky thing, to admit where you might have had some lucky breaks too; it's all part of the journey.

'Work' comes in many different shapes and guises, and if just hard work equals millions of pounds, then all nurses on night shifts would be millionaires. Yes, the Kardashians may have been *savvier* in some ways entrepreneurially, but this is different to getting up and *working*. Many, many people in society work extremely hard, so it's really difficult to hear such simplistic comments around success and hard work. When people believe all their success is just down to hard work, a blame culture starts to emerge, which implies that anyone who doesn't reach the lofty heights of success just can't have been using their twenty-four hours well enough or working hard enough. It glosses over the cracks and problems within society and economics at large.

Hashi Mohamed's story of arriving in Britain as a

child-refugee to then becoming a barrister at No5 Barristers Chambers in London gives him a unique perspective on this. His is a journey of success against the odds. The blurb of his book asks: 'What does it take to make it in modern Britain? Ask a politician, and they'll tell you it's hard work. Ask a millionaire, and they'll tell you it's talent. Ask a CEO and they'll tell you it's dedication. But what if none of those things is enough?' I wanted to ask Hashi about why he felt it was important to share his story, as he is very clear that the message, 'Well, if X did this, we ALL can' can be quite a damaging narrative. On my podcast he explained that people are being given wrong assumptions and wrong ideas about what it means to succeed, as they're only hearing from a small number of examples. 'Stories like mine, or other self-made stories, are effectively used by the minority of people who've succeeded based on the parameters that we live in, and they're used to beat people over the head,' he said. He also explained that we don't pay attention to the uncontrollable factors around success enough and gave the example of how 'the extortionate amount of money' paid to hardworking footballers, basketball players, Formula One drivers, senior banking executives and rich lawyers, for example, is very much a modern phenomenon. While those kinds of salaries might be seen as the ultimate success story today, going back centuries, none of these jobs would have existed in the same way, with the status and money that come with them. Therefore luck, timing and environment all have something to do with it.

In our current climate, someone talented and hardworking like Molly-Mae can do very well, but those opportunities could have also fallen to someone else just like her. I think similarly about my career. I have worked hard, and I must have some talent, but I believe there is also an element that we can't quite put our finger on. This is not me dismissing my success but interrogating it, as I feel many of us should. Why me? Is it purely down to luck? I got up every day and 'worked' like Kim Kardashian, and I wrote every night when I was starting out. But that is not unique. There are people out there who work harder than I do, and are more talented than I am, who haven't got to where I have. The formula is not clear.

I also asked Hashi about which factors he thinks make the most difference in this roulette of luck and privilege, hard work and talent. Can we ever pinpoint how or why someone has become successful? Is it an impossible task? He told me about a professor at Cornell University called Robert Franks who explains the role of luck in life in his book *Success and Luck: Good Fortune and the Myth of Meritocracy*. 'He advises never to mention luck in the presence of self-made men, because a lot of self-made men will ardently and vociferously say it's got nothing to do with luck. He explains that luck is a bit like when you're riding a bicycle up a hill, when the wind is against you, and every single bone and muscle in your body is working hard to go up this hill. You feel like bad luck is pushing you back. It's making all your muscles work, it's really, really straining you. You take a left or a right, and now you're on a decline, cycling downwards, the wind is at your back, your muscles are not working as hard, but you are flying down that path compared to where you were just a few moments ago. That's an example of good luck.' He continues with Franks' analogy: 'A few seconds after you've turned the corner, you won't really notice it any more. You're much more likely to say that it's all you doing the hard work cycling down this hill.' It explains why in our daily lives and society, we are much more likely to be aware of our bad luck because it's in our faces, and we have a negativity bias that makes us more likely to remember bad things happening to us. It's repetitive, and it's persistent. 'The moment we have good luck,' Hashi says, 'we are much more likely to ignore it, or discount it, and much more likely to believe that it's down to our hard work and our determination.' It's true. I admit that when things go well, I tend to assume it's because of a decision I made – and when things go wrong, there is a moment when I try and find an external justification first.

Looking back, something that I think was meant to empower women has actually been damaging to our notions of success. Growing up, we were encouraged to own our achievements, never to downplay ourselves, and didn't ever stop to think about where luck might have come into it. 'Girls, you're not lucky, you've worked HARD!' an old editor of a magazine once said to her junior staff in a meeting room. We were banned from saying we were lucky. But now I can acknowledge my luck for sure – and I can also say my luck created more luck. My work created more work. My privilege stems from a combination of factors: socio-economic advantages, supportive parents (emotionally, and financially in the first year I moved to London); experiences of both state and private education; encouragement from wider family members; an innate passion for writing; a supportive partner, which have all led to a robust inner confidence. All these things are privileges, or lucky breaks, whatever you want to call them. It doesn't harm me to share them, or help anybody if I keep them hidden away. It doesn't take away from anything I have achieved. It would be wrong not to admit that they exist and be honest about how they play a role in my 'success'.

Each of us has our own set of privileges. The circumstances we grow up in can help or hinder, depending on the lens you look at them through. For some people, living in a nice house enables them to have the comfort to work from home in a job they like. Some people could find that living in a house they don't like is a strong motivator for them to change their situation. Some people might thrive being single and have more freedom to be ambitious; some people may find that there is privilege in having the support of a partner. Some people are successful because they had no support from their parents and had to work harder, and some people are successful because they had emotional or financial support from their parents. It's not clear-cut. Our individual motivations and goals are not the same.

We all have privileges we probably never really think much about. A *British Medical Journal* study stated that you were more likely to be successful if you were taller. Research published in the *Oxford Bulletin of Economics and Statistics* reveals that easy to pronounce and common names are the most likely to get to the interview stage, i.e. it was found that a Chinese candidate must submit 68 per cent more applications than a potential employee with a Western-sounding name.

The important thing is to acknowledge where you got help, where you benefited, where you got a leg-up on the ladder – and then hopefully you will use that knowledge to help others by dint of being transparent. If success is something that can come more easily to you (i.e. you do not experience the barriers of sexism, ableism or racism), then you will likely be more relaxed about your own measures of success, as you have more avenues open to you, earlier on in your career. In her popular newsletter *Agents & Books*, literary agent Kate McKean spoke about the different hurdles for authors, remarking: 'It is easier for more white people to be ¯_(ツ)_/¯ (shrug) about sales or advances than marginalized people or people of colour. Most marginalized people and people of colour are held to a *much* higher standard when it comes to sales and measuring success and, on the flip side, it's assumed that certain topics or stories will not meet even modest levels of success from the jump.'

If you are on the back foot in terms of having agency over your career, you might not be so laid back about how a piece of work performs. The stakes might be higher for one employee than for another, and they might *need* a project to be successful for financial reasons, rather than for emotional or personal ones. You might not be able to relax your hours or work part-time because you need every penny you can get. It is important to inspect and be aware of this, and be transparent about the things that contributed to our own personal successes. We are all equal, but we are not the same. It's important to acknowledge that we don't live in a meritocracy. But there is good news: there are some things we can do, and mindsets we can adopt, to even out the disparity and plot our own course to a more successful life. We can decide to sit firmly in the driver's seat of our own lives and do what we can.

Despite the chasms in our society, the internet has certainly moved the goalposts when it comes to creating a more democratic playing field. Thanks to emerging technology, open platforms and the decreasing power of gatekeepers, we now have more access to opportunity than ever. There are more ways in which we can make a difference or start something new, without permission from the traditional decision-makers.

So, while traditionally nepotism has been a big contributor to success, nowadays it doesn't have to be about who you know, but manipulating the way knowledge is passed on to you.

It's Who You (Sort of) Know

In his *Times* piece, 'Why success in life is the art of the possible', James Marriott lays out an argument as to why 'imaginative proximity' is a key to success. Being near to someone who is successful, or knowing someone who is successful in what they do, can inspire you to believe it's possible for you too. The smallest sprinkling of inspiration can be the gateway, the first step, the sowing of a tiny seed. But if you have never come across anyone who shows you what success really looks like, then you may never have let yourself imagine or dream it to be a possibility for yourself. It's the classic 'you have to see it, to believe it'. He uses the examples of Barack Obama's father being a politician in Kenya setting him on the path to the White House, and Morrissey being physically close to the Manchester music scene inspiring him to record his own music.

In terms of my own life, I would say there is truth in this, of how influenced you can be by the people near to you. I had heard the story countless times of my dad quitting his job and taking an element of financial risk to set up his own business. A success story of someone taking a leap of faith and making it on their own was lodged deep inside my brain. At the end of his article, Marriott writes: 'Of course, most success requires money, contacts, intelligence or the nepotistic intervention of powerful relatives. But without those advantages, imagination is not useless.' But even if you don't have those elusive connections, the internet has made it so much easier to find like-minded individuals and ideas to help spark your imagination. It has collapsed the distance between us, and help from 'a friend of a friend of a friend' can change the course of your life. Viewing images online or listening to interviews can allow us to dream bigger. It is more likely nowadays that a seed will be planted in our minds. It's more satisfying to go out and make your own connections than to wait for opportunities to fall into your lap, anyway.

Nepotism irritates people for good reason: of course it feels unfair. The term 'nepo baby' trends regularly on TikTok, when people are surprised when they learn their favourite Gen Z actor has famous Hollywood parents. While it's true that traditional nepotism can lead to 'success' on paper, it's not necessarily all fun and games down that path. In Lily Allen's 2018 memoir *My Thoughts Exactly*, she interrogates the tension between nepotism and success, and explains how she wanted to achieve in spite of who her parents are, not because of them. Describing the West London kids-of-super-rich-people she'd hang out with, she says, 'They all seemed to share the unmistakable combination of jaded entitlement and debilitating lack of purpose that marks out trust-fund kids.' For true fulfilment, you need the proximity to success, and the desire to make it on your own. Nepotism is definitely a route in, but it cannot sustain an entire career by itself. That is a myth.

Being a famous person's child doesn't sound all that good, in fact. In a 1995 piece in *Psychology Today*, Mary Loftus lays out the few pros and many cons. She mentions 'Dysgradia, a syndrome where there is a complete lack of connection between doing and getting', sufferers of which find nothing inherently motivating, because whether they work hard or not, they'll still have access to everything they could ever need. Their 'success' is *inherited* through nepotism. It is not actually theirs. This can make people feel unworthy, and, in turn, ironically, not very successful in their own right. Brooklyn Beckham's photography book wasn't judged solely as a creative project: he was immediately described across the press as 'son of ex-footballer David and fashion designer Victoria Beckham'. Opinions of the book aside, it is hard to separate out the artist from the stepping stone, and you can't ignore the fact that he didn't earn his stripes in the same way as other creatives. Nepotism and privilege can of course make life easier in terms of material comforts and a quicker path to the 'top', but that might not translate to satisfaction. Most of us would agree we'd like to achieve our goals on our own terms. So even if you may feel further behind the starting line than those who have a leg-up, the path to success may well feel more fulfilling.

Youth Has No Age

The idea of youth as a privilege is constantly sold to us. Anti-ageing products are everywhere. Once we are no longer fresh-faced and starry-eyed, we are made to feel as though we are on the back foot because of our age – and it's not just paranoia. We all know facts like Oscar-winning film director Damien Chazelle was only thirty-two when he won Best Director for *La La Land*; Zadie Smith wrote *White Teeth* aged twenty-one; and Millie Bobbie Brown had eighteen million followers by the time she was fourteen. Don't get me wrong, highlighting the work of young people is extremely important, especially when it comes to activism, amplifying voices and making change. In a world that still loves stringent hierarchy and a society which judges young people for their apparent narcissism and selfies, we need to celebrate teenagers like Amika George, the founder of Free Periods, X Gonzalez, an American advocate for gun control, and Malala Yousafzai, who have inspired millions around the globe to strive for better. But for so long, society has celebrated and fetishized youth, when really, we are only getting started when we are young. And this has dangerous results: according to CV-Library, 85.3 per cent of those aged fifty-five to sixty-four say they've faced age discrimination in the workplace.

For years, the Forbes 30 Under 30 list has been the definition of shiny millennial success. But recently, more and more people have openly admitted their contempt for it. In 2018, when I was twenty-eight, I remember staying up the night before the Forbes announcement, as I knew the list was going live at a minute past midnight. I was so excited at the prospect of making the list I couldn't sleep, and I was thinking that if my name appeared, *my whole life will change in an instant*. And then the page refreshed and there it was: 'Emma Gannon'.

When I was invited to the Forbes 30 Under 30 celebratory party for 'list-makers' in London I was nervous about attending, but I was also excited to go. I was a little sceptical, but I knew that this looked outwardly 'impressive' and would help me attract new clients. I took someone who works on my team for some camaraderie, as I knew we'd face a whole load of 'What do you do?' questions that always feel transactional rather than connective when you're mingling with strangers. When we arrived at the dimly lit swanky bar in Soho, we put our coats away and made our way through the groups of people chatting with cocktails. We stood by ourselves and said hi to a few people I vaguely knew. We went into the photobooth to kill some time and took some silly posed photos. A man then took to the stage, telling us through a microphone in an American accent that we were 'badasses' and 'hot cool things' and that we would 'take over the world'. We were the lucky ones, allowed into the special club, treated as an elite group of people, and it made me feel icky. I went home that night, sat on the sofa with my now-husband and honestly thought, *What the hell was that?* It was just a lot of random people in a bar getting drunk. It just wasn't really . . . real. I didn't feel any true connection at all. I don't think you're meant to talk about how flat it actually feels to make it on to an arbitrary 'list'. To be slapped on the back, and for someone to say: 'Well done, we [the gatekeepers of the list] validate you now.' You realize, after all that, it wasn't *that* kind of validation you were looking for. A 'list' is not the moment you feel full up. No amount of outside approval actually scratches the itch. The itch comes back. Validation has to come from somewhere else, somewhere more meaningful.

At thirty, you are just getting started. You really are. We all know that great things can take a long time to grow, distil, ripen, mature or evolve. In a world of instant gratification and 'content', I don't think we should be celebrating whoever got there the quickest. That sounds like a race to the bottom, in fact. And I'm not alone. Erik Hoel shared a similar experience in his article, 'Forbes 30 Under 30 is an awkward ego-fest', which suggests that the list isn't just about celebrating success; it's also a very good marketing tool . . . for Forbes.

I am not afraid of ageing; in fact, I'm embracing it. Creatives and artists in particular tend only to get better with age. A few years back, I made a mini audio documentary for the Tate and travelled to St Ives to explore the artists who made waves there, such as Barbara Hepworth. As part of my research, I went looking for painter Alfred Wallis's grave up on the Barnoon cemetery that overlooks the beach. His grave stands out, as since he didn't make much money from his work, his friends clubbed together to give him an elaborate send-off. The tombstone is covered by beautifully painted tiles which portray somebody entering a lighthouse, symbolizing the end of life. The Tate in St Ives has celebrated his work loudly and proudly, and his paintings will be memorialized for many more years to come. But I later learned that he only began to take up painting in his seventies. It's *never* too late.

The Magnetism of a Contrarian

As I've outlined above, there is no such thing as a success formula because we are all different people on our own paths, and sometimes the odds are not stacked in our favour (or, in some cases, they are). One of the big 'aha' moments I got from interviewing more than four hundred podcast guests, was that none of them followed a set formula, and instead they use a blend of their unique qualities and perspectives to help them achieve great things. I thought I'd be able to glean the 'answer' to shiny success from my guests, but I ended up realizing that there isn't just one route, and that many of my assumptions were in fact myths (hence I'm writing this book).

But despite their differences, I did notice a commonality. By flying in the face of traditional wisdom, by having a different viewpoint on things, by being contrarian, they have stood out from the crowd and opened themselves up to opportunity. In the dictionary, a contrarian is defined as 'a person who opposes or rejects popular opinion'. It's a person who, for whatever reason, just goes for it. I particularly like the definition by entrepreneur and investor Naval Ravikant: 'A contrarian isn't one who always objects – that's a conformist of a different sort. A contrarian reasons independently, from the ground up, and resists pressure to conform.' There is something about their confidence that propels them forwards into luck and success. This doesn't make them more talented or 'better' than anyone else, but they possess a state of mind that means they are more likely to try to succeed. They *believe* in the path they are taking. They feel compelled, they listen to their feelings, they follow their gut instincts. They are in tune with some sort of inner voice. Like the entrepreneur who dropped out of school to pursue his business idea, the contrarian attitude is also one of dogged persistence. But it is important to note that this doesn't mean persistence at any cost and working around the clock – and in some cases, of course, it doesn't work. But to be successful in your own life in whatever way you want means pushing back on other people's ideas about you, and pushing back on conforming with things that don't feel right to you. It's following that feeling in your body, in your bones, that is trying to tell you which direction to go. This is why many successful people are often told at first that they are a bit 'out there' – because they are choosing a path that goes against people's expectations. They are often not taking the easy route. Often, people try and dissuade contrarians, because they would prefer them to come back to a place of safety.

Julia Cameron once said, 'Very often audacity – not talent – makes one person an artist and another person a shadow artist.' Swiss psychiatrist Carl Jung used the term 'shadow' in his work to describe aspects of those who do not fully embrace or acknowledge what they hold within them. Audacity is the opposite of how we're made to behave when we're young. We are told to follow the rules, to be quiet, to stop being annoying, to follow the path of life, get good grades, keep colouring within the lines, stay in our lane, stick to the straight and narrow, and then we'll be successful. If we do all this, we will get the job promotion, we will get to the place we want to go. But this couldn't be further from the truth. The irony is, the more you stay within the confines of what you think success is, the less likely you are to be very successful. It's thinking outside the box, moving away from other people's definitions of success, and spotting a unique opportunity that leads to the greatest rewards. It's the people who take a chance instead of hanging back, or take a different route when everyone else is gunning for yet another flash-in-the-pan trend. Successful people are usually opportunists. And crucially, they know themselves well enough to recognize when an opportunity is right for *them*, not just 'a good opportunity' in general.

Contrarians question everything and don't just go along with things. I know what you might be thinking: we can't *all* be contrarians; the world would fall apart. Of course, there are the rare, overtly successful contrarian types like Elon Musk, but not everyone can be as extreme as this, nor should they want to be (!). But it's not about being an extreme contrarian. It's about taking a small pinch of this characteristic and making small tweaks so that you are living a life better suited to you, your personality, your needs. Rebelling even ever so slightly against the rules or the things holding you back. Putting your needs higher up on the list. Defying the 'shoulds'. Even if we don't want to reach the dizzying heights of worldwide success or are scared of going against the tide every day, we can still take lessons from contrarians. We can all interrogate the motion of our days and change small things up. This could be as simple as suggesting a different way of running your meetings to your boss. Or asking to trial a four-day working week if you're self-employed. It could mean having an open relationship, or having a different kind of wedding, or deciding to move abroad, or making sure you have a daily walk to stretch your legs when working from home.

Being a contrarian in the way we live can make us feel more fulfilled and empowered in smaller ways. For example, saying no to something your family expect you to do, turning down something you know will make you stressed or ill, or deciding against something all your friends are doing – these seemingly small things can all lead us back to our true selves. It shouldn't be viewed as overly rebellious to go after what you want. We feel like we are going against the culture when we say no, or when we push back on what we 'should' want to go after or what we 'really' want. It's important to focus in on what *you* want and even share it, say it out loud or write it down. A study done by Dr Gail Matthews, a psychology professor at Dominican University of California, found that 'You become 42 per cent more likely to achieve your goals and dreams, simply by writing them down on a daily basis.'

But, importantly, being contrarian doesn't mean being overly selfish or self-centered. It's about taking innovative steps to improve things, on your own terms. Usually, when you improve your own life, you inspire people (without realizing) to improve theirs.

Some may think society would dissolve into total disarray if more people took small risks, but it's not necessarily the case. Instead, I think we'd become more entrepreneurial, and that society would benefit from that: from new inventions, suggestions or experimentations. I think we would be happier in our own lives and yes, it would benefit the economy too. New research from Kaspersky Lab reveals that a third of UK workers believe they would be closer to having their dream careers if they had taken more risks in the workplace. The people in this study know deep down that risks are worth taking, even if they don't ever take them: 45 per cent said they don't take enough risks in life, erring on the side of caution and see risk-taking as a negative trait. We live in a society that doesn't encourage us or set us up to take risks, so we tend to hold back. It's a vicious circle. We are often scared, for good, logical reasons, but it's overcoming those fears that is the hard and often worthwhile part. The irony is that humans are incredibly adaptable and are more capable during riskier times than we think we are. A 2018 Harvard Business School study showed that a large proportion (68 per cent) of executives who had been let go landed a new job within six months. An additional 24 per cent had a new job by the end of one year – plus, 91 per cent of executives who had been fired took a job of a similar or even greater level of seniority. I have heard countless examples of people doing great things after being made redundant. But it is those people who are brave enough to jump before they are pushed who often reap greater rewards. We tend to underestimate our adaptability and resilience, so we can find it hard to go against the grain. We tend to forget about all those times we happened to land on our feet.

Now that we've laid out some realities, how can we feel emboldened to take risks to move forward towards our own meaning of success? It is important to draw the distinction between something external standing in our way (like our lack of privilege), and when we are standing in our own way. We require a variety of tools to help us overcome different hurdles. Suffering from chronic fatigue syndrome is a totally different hurdle to dealing with impostor syndrome, for example. One is a real physical condition, and one stems from our thoughts. ACT (acceptance and commitment therapy) psychologists call these two types of obstacles/suffering 'clean' pain and 'dirty' pain. 'Clean' pain is what we feel when something hurtful happens to us. 'Dirty' pain is the feelings we have when our *thoughts* are hurtful to us. Contrarians are good at knowing the difference, able to separate out what is a real obstacle and what is a story we are telling ourselves.

When our thinking is the thing in the way of our next step, rather than an actual circumstance, this is called a 'limiting belief'. A limiting belief is a state of mind, or a thought that you are convinced is true, that limits or holds you back in some way. Most of us have limiting beliefs around our lives and what we are or are not capable of:

- 'I can't leave my job.'
- 'I'm not good enough.'
- 'I won't be able to find a better job.'
- 'I am stuck like this for ever.'

These are all thoughts, not facts. Certain beliefs become so embedded in our psyches that we take them as absolute fact. We do it all the time when judging other people without really realizing. We judge someone for being loud on the bus, cutting in the queue, or even make assumptions about them based on how they are dressed – thinking they are out to ruin *our* day. Our thoughts can turn into full-blown assumptions. But even when these thoughts feel like truths, there are often cracks which we can start to investigate to lead us to a plan, an escape route, or a way of changing things.

An acquaintance of mine recently sold all her belongings and travelled the world, *Eat Pray Love*-style. We were talking about this at a party, when a woman said, 'I wish I could do that, but I wouldn't be able to afford it.' My travelling friend explained that her backpack adventure was far cheaper than the way in which the woman at the party was currently living. She had sold her house and was staying on friends' sofas and in cheap lodgings. Not many people would sell their houses to do this, but it doesn't mean it's not possible. We could all do with taking a fresh look from time to time at the thoughts we hold about ourselves. Only then will we feel able to take the risks we need to, to be a contrarian (in whatever way that looks like to you – you could even be a contrarian against the idea of being a contrarian – meta!)

The behaviours and qualities I've noticed in successful contrarians include:

Slight outsiders: Whether it was being unpopular at school or feeling on the fringes of society in whatever way, they grew up feeling slightly outside the box. They felt a bit 'weird' but found a way to lean into it, and now explore these things that made them stand out.

Slight rule-breakers: People who find a way to succeed in their chosen field usually don't mind rebelling, or at least finding ways to bend the rules. They don't like being told what to do! This is at odds with the factory mentality of the obedient worker of the Industrial Revolution.

A focus on education: Education is at the heart of everything. Whether it was private school, or having great teachers, or home-schooling, or having been self-taught, they continue to learn endlessly, read lots, and see themselves as a perpetual student. They never feel 'done' with any topic and are always hunting for new information.

A fire in their belly: 'Passion' is an overused word and doesn't quite sum up the energy my guests emit. But something has lit them up, whether that's activism, caring about the future, a personal event from their past, or simply a clear reason to get up in the mornings. Their actions are deliberate, motivating them beyond just money and status.

Curiosity: Like curious children, all my guests ask a lot of questions, and don't just want to talk about themselves. They often ask others about their experiences and tend to poke the fire to find out why things are the way they are, and how we can do them differently. They question the 'rules' of the world.

A solid EQ: It's not a case of needing to be really smart IQ-wise, and knowing how to pass exams, it's more about being emotionally intelligent, getting on with others easily, and knowing how to 'read a room'. There is an inherent likeability to my guests, or at least a general respect towards them. Our energy matters, and what you put out into the world does seem to come back in some way. Being kind, sociable and interested in other people helps. Being rude and entitled caps your potential.

A sprinkling of self-doubt: Some may say that really successful people walk around with massive egos, never questioning their decisions, but from my experience, many people I have interviewed have a little nagging inner critic that constantly questions if they are doing the right thing. This makes them second-guess themselves but drives them further by encouraging them to try again and again until they have the best route.

A practice: Or consistency. Each of my guests has a consistent way of delivering their work to the world, whatever that looks like. Some may call it 'hard work' (or graft or grit) of some kind. There is a practice, process and professionalism behind the work, a groove: whether that's a routine, religion, belief or spirituality. Be they a heart-surgeon or a YouTuber, most successful people show up over and over again, and are consistent in their methods and in the daily work they do. They are committed.

Plus:

Talent, natural aptitude or skill: We are all born with a gift of some sort, which when nurtured can unlock great things, whether it's something specific like singing, styling, curating or coding, or broader abilities like being a good talker.

Privilege: Including, but not limited to, education, social class, age, nationality, geographic location, physical abilities, race, gender, gender identity, neurology, sexual orientation, physical attractiveness, and religion.

Luck: There's no denying that success or failure seemingly can be brought on by chance and mysterious factors we can't put our fingers on, rather than direct actions.

Now, you might have more of an idea of how to set yourself up to best achieve success, but that's useless if you're striving for the wrong thing. Often, we follow a map, well-intentioned and laid out by parents, family, schooling, society, but to tune in to what we *really* want, we need to check in with our inner compass. Just as there's no one way to achieve success, there's no one definition of success, and the following chapters will help you work out your own personal and authentic version.

Chapter Reflections

1. **What traits do you have that can set you up for success?** Do you have any contrarian elements to the way you live your life? Is there anything you want to change? If you are unsure how to identify your own traits, ask a few friends to give you three words that describe your most beloved qualities, and see what patterns you notice.

2. **In what areas of your life do you feel lucky?** We all have luck in our lives, even if it's not

immediately obvious. Can you take a moment here to recognize any of your own privileges by acknowledging a time (or few times) luck has gone your way? Even the smallest thing?

3. **In what circumstances have you made your own luck?** By doing something out of the blue, or experimenting, or making a change – when did this work out? What actions or decisions have led to more lucky breaks? What could you try next time?

4. **Can you name some of your limiting beliefs?** Write down some thoughts you have about why you might feel unsuccessful or what is currently standing in your way. For example, one of my limiting beliefs in the past has been: 'Other people are more talented than me.' (Later in the book you might want to come back to these with the new tools you pick up along the way.)

5. **If you could change one small thing about your life, what would it be?** Think of the smallest possible thing you could change. Include small contrarian scenarios into your life (e.g. a different way of doing something, like sending

emails at a different time of day or wearing a bolder item of clothing just because you want to). Experimenting with the smaller things can enable us to start thinking about trying bigger things.

6. **What does 'not having it all' look like to you?** What's one thing you could drop? What could you take away? What makes your shoulders relax?

TWO

The Happiness Myth

'It's very clear to me that success and happiness are two very different things – and after a lot of external success I've realized more of that isn't going to fill me in any sort of spiritual way.'

RUPI KAUR, ON *TALK EASY* PODCAST

A man in the street yelled at me the other day to smile. Reader, I did not smile. Being told to 'cheer up, love' is a very common occurrence, especially if you are a woman minding your own business. When I am walking along, I am often deep in thought, or listening to a podcast, or planning my dinner, or reflecting on something inside the filing cabinets of my mind. I DON'T WANT TO SMILE. There is something about a woman not smiling that seems to rile people up.

Of course, this isn't exclusive to women: men also have their emotions policed; they are told to put on a brave face, to 'provide' and 'be strong', even when what they might really need is an opportunity to crumble on to someone and feel their feelings. I don't need to remind you that suicide is the biggest killer of men under the age of fifty. 'Putting on a brave face' can be a seriously damaging concept.

Across the whole of our society, in many different ways, there is something deeply wrong with the way we tell people to buck up and be happy. Happiness is a word used as a blanket term for feeling good. In the dictionary it says: *Happiness is an emotional state characterized by feelings of joy, satisfaction, contentment, and fulfilment.* So many of us are trapped in the ways we are 'supposed' to feel. But when do we actually question the things in life that give us satisfaction in the moment? Most of the time the things I think should give me joy actually don't, whereas the things I overlook as boring or familiar or small give me huge dollops of joy. For example, getting attention on social media often makes me feel flat (I always assume I'd feel happy with more likes), yet conversation when a good friend calls me out of the blue, when I'm convinced I'm too busy, instantly cheers me up. Science backs this up, with differing brain chemicals involved in our emotions when connecting loosely online, compared with when we have direct human interaction. Creativity makes me feel free, because when I am writing or making, I am not overthinking (and I'm using the right side of my brain, which is associated with being more visual and intuitive.)

This chapter is all about unpicking those 'shoulds' and looking at how the happiness ideal keeps us trapped. I want to explore how we can attempt to break free from our culture's insistence on 'happy-washing' or 'toxic positivity': a pervasive condition of outward smiles and faux happiness.

While we might think that obsessing over our emotions is a modern affliction, it's nothing new. In the sixteenth century, according to *Idler*, 'melancholia', rather than happiness, was the 'signature sickness of the time' and 'a condition of the soul'. People would actually feel smug about their suffering, like they had managed to 'feel' their way into something important, and would write poetry and art from this place of 'higher consciousness'. Nowadays, the same premium is placed on happiness, but this overwhelming insistence on false happiness is even more stark when we consider it in the context of our current, often still hidden, mental health crisis. It feels like an endless performance of 'Look how happy I am.'

For a nation obsessed with the concept of happiness, ironically, we've never been more anxious or depressed. One in seven people in England now takes an antidepressant, according to the latest NHS data. A 2018 study from the Mental Health Foundation found that 74 per cent of UK adults have felt 'so stressed at some point over the last year they felt overwhelmed or unable to cope', and that was before the Covid-19 pandemic. In the US, there is a teenage mental health crisis, according to a new Centers for Disease Control and Prevention study which states that over the past ten years, 'persistent feelings of sadness or hopelessness' in teenagers rose from 26 per cent to 44 per cent, the highest level of teenage sadness ever recorded. A 2020 study by Investors in People found that 60 per cent of all UK workers are unhappy at work. We normalize this crisis with 'I Hate Mondays' merchandise, memes of grumpy cats, and pop songs about living for the weekend. Until we get to the root of why society as a whole is unhappy and hurting, and why we're all pretending we're totally fine when we're not, sadly this will continue in a vicious cycle.

We often assume that if someone has everything, then they obviously live a charmed life. I am guilty of looking at someone's life on Instagram and thinking, *their life looks perfect* and assuming they have absolutely nothing challenging going on. Of course, this is hardly ever the case. Actor Selena Gomez recently sat down with President Joe Biden to discuss the issue of mental health, speaking candidly about her own. You might assume that someone like her (rich, famous, beautiful, with 336 million followers on Instagram) wouldn't struggle, until you dig deeper and discover that she lives with bipolar disorder, as well as lupus, and has undergone a kidney transplant and chemotherapy. The image she projects doesn't necessarily reflect what's going on inside. Tragic reminders of this fact are seen far too often. I try not to check the news first thing in the morning, but one day a news story about a woman who had taken her own life was sadly trending on Twitter. Cheslie Kryst was the beautiful winner of Miss USA in 2019, a successful lawyer who had also worked on an Emmy-nominated entertainment show and was signed to one of the world's largest talent agencies. We don't know the full story, but it was incredibly tragic to read about. If simply becoming 'successful' was the answer to life's problems, then tragic things like this just wouldn't happen. But we know it's not as simple as that. Mental health problems do not discriminate. We can see this proven time and time again: a list of achievements certainly does not guarantee you'll be immune from suffering. The narrative of fame, beauty and achievements magically making life better should not be so pervasive, yet for some reason, despite all proof, it persists.

The tools in this chapter are designed to help us accept life's ups and downs, but they are not a solution to any kind of mental health issue – please do prioritize your wellbeing and seek professional help if necessary. Having support and therapy can improve our lives, but we shouldn't also assume success can only be achieved when we are mentally well. We can find a way to move towards our goals at a pace that suits us, and living in harmony with the truths of our lives can lead to our biggest breakthroughs. We don't have to cover up who we are and we can succeed in our own way. There's no denying it is incredibly hard navigating life's challenges, and there are many things on our path to success that we can only see in hindsight once we begin to recover.

Describing Happiness

On a recent trip to Copenhagen, I sat on a bench in the Tivoli Gardens with an ice cream in hand, my husband sat next to me, children (other people's) feeding the ducks, the sun beating down on my face, music playing and the smell of doughnuts wafting my way. In that moment I could understand why Denmark is reported to be one of the happiest places in the world. I looked around and felt like I was in a kids' TV show. Gondola-style boats were floating on the water, blossom was budding on the trees, people were lying back on deckchairs, and an endless blue sky stretched up above. But when I really try to pinpoint my feelings sitting on that bench, I wouldn't necessarily say I was happy with a capital H. 'Happiness' feels too grand, something all-encompassing, a permanent state of being. Instead, I was feeling a moment of joy. Bliss. The sun on my face.

Many of us have the idea that one day we will crack the happiness code, that once we make it, we will reach an everlasting state of contentment. *I'll be happy* when. *I'll be happy* if. That *will make me happy,* when *I get there*. Happiness is used in the context of the future a lot – but I've found that in the present moment it feels more like joy, and it's OK if it is fleeting. In fact, it makes it all the more sweet. For me, it's noticing these momentary joyful occasions that has added so much to my life: stopping to really notice those moments like the one in Copenhagen; feeling it all in that instant, being really present for it, rather than already chasing the next moment, or worrying it's all about to end. Unbreakable unwavering happiness no longer feels like the goal, so instead I want to savour the moments of it, those ones that land on you like a fluttering butterfly, and then fly off again.

We can be confused about happiness because the ways we have to talk about it are too limited. Therefore, our over-simplistic expectations aren't lining up with reality. Sometimes human language can't convey our emotions. I have an app on my phone which plays me the soft voices of kind people guiding me through meditations when I need to take a moment to pause. At the end of the ten minutes, I can rate my mood. The options span 'Awful', 'Bad', 'Okay', 'Great', 'Happy'. I find myself clicking 'Okay' or 'Great' more often than 'Happy'. It makes me wonder what 'happy' even means. These words just don't sum it up. Sometimes I do just feel OK. *Fine! Good!* Nothing is going terribly wrong! Feelings of sheer happiness and joy are fleeting, saved for the dopamine rushes of big sweeping moments.

There are so many other more interesting human emotions than just happiness. Excitement. Relief. Love. Pride. Amazement. Gratitude. Amusement. Hope. What is happiness supposed to feel like? That giddiness of running through a field? Laughing at a sausage dog on YouTube? A child jumping in a puddle? I often have to remind myself that fun and happiness are different things. As author and former Google engineer Mo Gawdat explains: 'So I'm at a party, I'm jumping up and down, I have a couple of drinks, am I happy? No, I'm having fun. This is very different. Having fun, in that case, is a brief moment, I call it the *state of escape*. Believe it or not, it's not a state of happiness.' Having fun is great – but it's not going to magically turn into happiness if we chase fun constantly. Happiness is not something we need to force; we're more likely to feel happy-like feelings if we actually take the pressure off ourselves first. Ultimately happiness can't be bottled and bought and sold – the *idea* of happiness can be, though, and it makes companies billions of dollars.

I Hope this Finds You Well

Beyond feelings of fun, contentment, excitement and fleeting happiness, there are of course more difficult emotions to contend with. A friend recently messaged me saying: 'I will NOT start the email hoping it "finds you well" as I am sure, like all of the human population, this email finds you feeling about a thousand emotions on average each day!' I really liked how the expectation was lifted from the usual 'hope you're DOING REALLY WELL' opener. Sometimes we just aren't feeling well or happy, because life is hard, and our brains aren't wired to be continuously jolly, as most of the time they are just trying to keep us alive. Sometimes, we are quite simply not having a great day.

Society wants us to pretend to be happy all the time (because it's more comfortable for everyone, especially employers) while simultaneously selling us happiness cures. It all just reinforces the happiness myth. But an article in the *Scientific American* even suggests that so-called negative emotions could be key to our wellbeing: '[they] most likely aid in our survival. Bad feelings can be vital clues that a health issue, relationship or other important matter needs attention. The survival value of negative thoughts and emotions may help explain why suppressing them is so fruitless.' Our brains are wired to pay attention to them, so trying to push them away, as toxic positivity demands, is physiologically impossible.

I'm not for one moment saying depression or severe negative feelings are 'good'. I'm saying there are so many grey areas in between 'happy' and 'sad' that are the shades that make up a colourful life. As Susan Cain argues in her book *Bittersweet*, sorrow, longing, melancholy and vulnerability are the things that actually make us whole. We shouldn't be ashamed of all the other emotions that don't fall under the category of 'happy'. If anything, we should lean into them, notice them, respect them and be curious about them. I'm starting to accept the ebb and flow of my moods and days and welcome them in. What if feeling the spectrum of human emotions means you are really living your life, in all its bright technicolour?

When I spoke to Dr Rafa Euba, a consultant psychiatrist based in London, I asked him about this medley of emotions we all seem to have. He said, 'We react to a permanently changing environment. It is simply impossible to disentangle the fear from the fun of a roller coaster, or the sadness from the sweet nostalgia in a sentimental song or the apprehension from the anticipation in an adventure.' So many personal examples spring to mind. My husband, Paul, recently found some old photos of us on a hard drive. As we went through them reminiscing, I felt so *happy* remembering what a good time we had in our twenties, and so grateful for the ten years of happiness of our relationship. So why did I then feel like crying just two seconds after this burst of joy? I suddenly felt viscerally sad. I realized it's because we will never get those old times back again: our old flat, our old freedoms, our old haircuts! I felt simultaneously happy looking back and totally flat, realizing we would never be *that* young again. But it's normal to feel such a mix of emotions. We can be grateful for what we have while mourning the things that now exist in the past.

I remember seeing a caption on Instagram from someone who said she had to attend a funeral, and therefore her day turned a bit 'negative'. Perhaps it was meant to be darkly funny, and we all grieve differently, but it was strange to see someone describe something as serious as a funeral as 'bad vibes', as if it was a blip in an otherwise perfect day. Feeling sad is not 'negative energy'. If we embrace our strong emotions, rather than trying to run away from them, we can learn and grow from our moments of sadness and discomfort. When I sat with author Clover Stroud recently to record an episode of my podcast, we were talking about the toxic nature of trying to force and perform happiness all the time. She has been through real challenges in her life: huge grief, tragedy and trauma from an early age, losing her mum and then losing her sister to breast cancer. She speaks of the spectrum of human emotions and how they have added huge things to her life: 'Creatively, grief is an interesting place to be. We learn much from our suffering and losses. I'm interested in the many different edges of that crystal, of the more challenging moments in our life.' She enjoys the bright technicolour of life, the sharp edges, the vividness, the melancholy and the meaning. 'Happiness is actually quite boring,' she said. Sometimes, it can be even weirdly enjoyable to listen to a melancholic soundtrack and lean into those feelings of sadness. When we embrace them and accept them as valid and real, they are more likely to lift. When we try and grip happiness too hard, or force 'bad' feelings to go away, we can make them feel worse.

I've also seen this dynamic play out in moments I think I'll enjoy. I've often felt like I should be happier or more excited when I'm doing a speaking event or experiencing a big personal moment (like my wedding day) that feels important. It's usually something I've agreed to because I'm looking forward to it and I want to do it. But then the nerves hit. Sometimes I feel anxious, all sick and scared. But it's not one or the other: I feel sick, scared, excited AND happy. It's even the case with huge, life-changing events. A friend of mine who has overcome serious health issues tells me that they are happy to be out of the woods, but they are also feeling a million other emotions at the same time: sadness, survivor's guilt and confusion. Well-meaning people say to her: 'You must be so *happy* you are out of hospital!' Well, it's often a lot more complicated than that. 'Success' doesn't mean papering over the cracks, or putting on a 'brave face', or pretending everything is fine. Success is remaining present in the difficult and joyous moments of life (and they're often one and the same, as meaningful moments often don't feel purely happy), accepting and being in tune with the reality, and learning to be OK with every version of yourself along the way, no matter how you feel.

Given that our emotions are so intertwined, we don't need to hang good and bad labels on absolutely everything. I am starting to enjoy feeling the flow of my emotions without placing morality on to them. I've stopped thinking that happy is 'good' and sad is 'bad'. Our brains are wired to keep us alive, which involves processing a number of different emotions, not to make us blissfully happy all the time. Dr Euba argues that the idea of permanent happiness is a construct invented by the 'positive thinking' industry: 'There are moments of fleeting joy that are not meant to be constant. And they're not meant to be that frequent, necessarily. We will never achieve a state of permanent joy.'

It's all well and good knowing this, but how can we break free from this collective ingrained habit of pretending everything is fine? How do we learn to embrace the negative emotions when they arise, rather than dwelling on them or ignoring them completely? I always try to remember that the physiological lifespan of an emotion in the body and brain is only ninety seconds. However, we can find ourselves in a loop and it can be so hard to get out of it. Neuroanatomist, author and public speaker Jill Bolte Taylor explains in her book *My Stroke of Insight: A Brain Scientist's Personal Journey* that it's only once we combine our emotions or anxieties with our inner thoughts, judgements on the world and internal belief systems that they become our 'feelings'. And then feelings that are maintained over hours or days become our mood. Feelings that linger over weeks or months become our temperament. If they last for years, they become a personality trait.

You'll know from experience that it's not the positive emotions that linger, but instead the spiralling loop of negative emotions. As humans, we have a natural bias towards the negative. We tend to remember traumatic experiences more clearly than positive ones, remember insults over praise, react more strongly to negative triggers than positive ones, ruminate about unhappy memories over happier ones, and so on. I asked Dr Euba to elaborate on this negativity bias, and why is it that we humans are so prone to scan things for negativity or danger? Why do we hang on to the one negative comment, in a sea of positivity? 'From a strictly natural perspective, we need to be aware of anything that is wrong in our environment. And therefore, when everything is fine, we are all right, our health, house and environment appears to be well, we still find something that is not quite right. In my book, I use the example of me forgetting the huge amount of things in my life that are absolutely fine, and focusing completely on a little crack in my wall that I'd found. Things like that get in the way of us feeling relaxed and happy about our existence. But that's the way we are designed.' Understanding that our negative emotions are a natural response can be a way to help us cope with overwhelming fears and moments of worry. But we can still get stuck if we don't have the tools to break the cycle of ruminating and overthinking.

It's important to learn ways in which we can be more in tune with the realities of our lives. *What parts are going well? Are you being unnecessarily hard on yourself? Have you achieved more than you think you have? Have you overcome a setback recently? Are you more resilient than you give yourself credit for? Have you had a small win?*

★

I nearly got a tattoo of a lizard recently. I'm glad I didn't, in hindsight, but I have fallen in love with the little reptile in my head. I first read about the lizard part of our brain a while ago, but getting to grips with it was a different story. This ancient part of the brain is called the amygdala, also known as the reptilian brain. It is in charge of fight, flight, feeding, fear, freezing up and fornication, and it controls our very basic reactions and functions. It is the primitive part of our brain that overreacts when it thinks we are in danger. Our lizard brain wants to protect us, but it often gets things a bit wrong. While our rational mind knows there is not a grizzly bear about to eat us outside the hotel room door, that our lives will not be ruined if we do a public talk on stage, that our best friend probably doesn't hate us just because she hasn't replied to our text yet, our lizard brain jumps to those conclusions. In our modern, fast-paced world, it's important to be aware of this disconnect. Just because our brains are acting scared, it doesn't mean that there's anything actually wrong. I have now named my lizard so that my anxious emotions feel slightly more distanced from my thoughts, and don't become part of this negative spiralling (she's called Allegra – don't ask).

The surface of who we are (our personality) is made up of all the thoughts that run through our heads, so in order to make change happen, we have to do the work to adjust our thoughts. Some thoughts are so embedded that it is surprising when we realize that they are just our thoughts, and not 'us'. The good news is: any one of us can change our thoughts, and any one of us can change our lives. Now, when Allegra tells me my book will be a failure, or there's a shark in the swimming pool, or that I left the oven on, when I checked it a million times, I can say, *Thanks Allegra, but I can take things from here.*

Instead of a tattoo, I have a gold necklace with a tiny lizard on it, to remind myself that when I feel like I'm in crisis, it is sometimes just my lizard brain acting out. It's just the ancient parts of my brain wanting to protect me, and I've accepted that my overreactive, dramatic lizard brain is not in charge of making me happy. By distancing myself from that part of my brain, I'm not reacting to its demands, which makes me feel less anxious and stops me defining my mood or my personality by it. When we talk about success, a huge part of stepping towards your goals, whatever they may be, is tweaking your internal dialogue and learning not to trust it as gospel. By being kinder to myself, and by turning down the volume of Allegra, I have built more self-compassion. I am more likely to continue with my grand plans, because I am on my own side. I am able to listen more deeply to the rational side of myself.

The more I talk to psychologists, the more I'm realizing that a big part of success is managing the negative emotions as they arise, as well as the good ones. It's about self-acceptance, kind self-talk and appreciating that life is not perfect.

If our brains can change, we can change. Nobody knows this better than Mo Gawdat, who revolutionized the conversation around being happy. (He calls his inner lizard 'Becky'.) Being a former engineer, he comes at the topic from a mathematical standpoint, and felt called to research and discuss happiness following the sudden, tragic death of his son. He has created a happiness equation, which is: *Your happiness is equal to or greater than the difference between the events of your life and your expectations of how life should behave.*

When I asked Mo if the key to happiness really was as simple as learning to look at things differently, he said, 'If it rains, are you happy or unhappy? It depends. If you want to water your plant, you will be happy. If you want to sit in the sun, you will be unhappy. And we constantly make these comparisons, leading us to feel happy or unhappy, simply depending on that difference of thought in our head.'

I wanted to see if I could simply 'be happier' from the minute I woke up, by changing up my thoughts and reframing them.

Morning thought: I wake up and think, *I'm tired.*
Morning thought reframed: *I am tired because I've been working hard on this book recently, and I'm enjoying*

*writing it and proud of myself for how much work I've done
on it.*

Lunchtime thought: *I am tired and annoyed at myself for
dropping my salad on the floor. How stupid could I be?!*
Lunchtime thought reframed: *How lucky am I that I
can make another lunch? It's annoying, but it's absolutely
fine.*

Evening thought: *It's raining and my umbrella has
broken. Everything goes wrong. Even my umbrella. I don't
want to live in a rainy city.* I question my whole life and
identity because of the cold, wet weather. *Why do I live
in a cold and rainy city? Do other people have it better in
warmer climes?*
Evening thought reframed: *Life is good here, and if I
lived in a sunny country, I don't think any of my problems
would vanish. In fact, I know I would miss my family and
miss the changing seasons. I write well on a rainy day and
find it cosy. It's OK, you're just annoyed that your umbrella
broke, let's go and eat some yummy food.*

This method acknowledges that something's gone wrong,
and in that way it's different to pretending everything is fine,
à la toxic positivity. I found that this worked well when

reframing the smaller, less important thoughts, and I did find it dramatically improved my day. It stops me spiralling unnecessarily. I could almost feel my brain whir and create new pathways separate to the go-to negativity that I would normally fixate on. Of course, we can't just 'reframe' every stressful, painful thing in our lives – especially if they are much bigger than these small moments I've mentioned here – but this thought experiment made my week so much more pleasant that I have carried on doing it to this day.

Reframing the thoughts that cause us suffering can powerfully change our relationship to success and happiness. It can help us appreciate the smaller things, and live our days with contentment, without our default always being about wanting more immediately. It is quite simply a perspective shift, a way to zoom in on your own life, without comparing and despairing in the context of everyone else's lives or being too harsh about our own.

Happiness isn't black-and-white: we can't put people into categories and say, 'You'll *always* be happy based on what you have,' or 'You'll *never* be happy based on what you have.' It doesn't work like that. I have interviewed and coached countless people who have lots of money, security, a great ocean view, but who are deeply depressed by their thoughts. I've also seen friends from school who left home at sixteen, got a job and never really wanted anything more than a simple life filled with friends, and who wake up each day grateful and happy with their lot. It doesn't always go this way, of course, and money and security definitely make people much more comfortable. But comfort is not the same as happiness (and I'll expand on this in the Money Myth chapter).

Simple Pleasures

In our modern Western world obsessed with capitalism and growth, there is an irony that many things we used to do in previous centuries to sustain ourselves (such as fishing, hunting, pottery and basket-weaving) are now things we do for fun, and for pleasure. We are trying to get back to nature in a hyper-commercial world, back to ourselves, back to some of the more simplistic elements of life.

When we plan too much into the future (I'll be happy *when*), we can neglect our present reality. I had a friend who used to spend all her time talking about her grand life plans. One day she was going to move to Australia, the next she was going to live in Singapore . . . no, actually, she'd get a new job in the UK. She spent two years talking about her five-year plan, which constantly changed, and then she fell in love and ended up living somewhere she had not ever imagined. There isn't a problem with daydreaming or planning, it can be really fun, and it's important to brainstorm openly about the life you want to live, but instead of creating a series of five-year plans, perhaps we should strip it back to find the small things that increase our chances of having better days in the here and now. Five-minute plans. Five-day plans. Five-week plans. Whatever works for you. After all, we can't predict where we'll end up. We don't even know for sure what tomorrow will bring. But we can find ways to make our everyday lives just that bit better.

If you can't be happy washing the dishes, you won't be happy having the nice cup of tea afterwards. If we can't be happy right now in whatever way possible, we won't be happy if all the things we ever wanted fall into our laps. Again, we might be healthier or more comfortable if that happens, but we are more likely to be happy *then* if we start with appreciating life as it is *now*.

Chapter Reflections

1. **How would you describe a small, joyful moment in your day?** When we turn towards joy and give our attention to it, we can start to pinpoint those parts of life (whether that's work

or home) that make us happiest. It's a strangely
simple tactic: do more of what makes you happy,
and less of what doesn't.

2. **What would your most perfect day look like if
    you had absolutely no barriers or obstacles?**
    Dream it, scheme it, write it down. Sow the seeds
    of the things that really make you feel joyful,
    without limiting yourself, even if it feels like a
    distant fantasy, and you might be surprised with
    what you uncover. Experiment with what
    elements you could integrate into your life now,
    even if they're tiny things.

3. **How does your lizard brain act and feel? Do
    they have a name, and what do they sound
    like?** My lizard brain (Allegra, as you already
    know) is very, very dramatic. When it feels like a
    fire alarm going off in my head, I know that is the
    moment to pause and analyze what is really
    going on, and whether it is my lizard brain
    speaking or if it is 'me'.

4. **What are some of your personal happiness
    myths? What did you think would make you
    happy but left you feeling differently once you**

had it? The feelings we get from achieving something that is meaningful to us are rarely just 'happiness': they're much more numerous and complex. (For example, I've never once heard a female friend only describe giving birth as 'happiness', or finishing a PhD as just 'happiness', but instead a whole range of beautiful, technicoloured emotions.) It's about defining them, naming them and moving away from needing to label everything as 'happiness' or for absolutely everything to be positive.

5. **What parts of 'ordinary life' make you feel warm and energized?** Write down the smallest things that bring you joy, and you'll see they are not so 'ordinary' after all. Notice how little money you need to do each of them, if any at all. If you can, factor more of this into every day.

THREE

The Productivity Myth

*'Listening to a podcast where a woman is talking
about how the key to getting everything done is
to get up at 4.45 a.m.'*

SIAN HARRIES, WRITER

Back in 1965, a Senate subcommittee in the US predicted our
working week would be reduced big time, and that we
would all be working around fourteen hours a week by the
year 2000, with at least seven weeks of holiday time, due to
the advances in technology. I hear a hollow laugh in the
background. Our modern life to-do list seems to be getting
longer, not shorter. We glamorize over-working. We move
on to the next thing without taking in what we've just done.
Our working day has increased by two hours since we began
having email on our phones (thanks to the invention of the

Blackberry/'crackberry'). Many friends tell me that it is a bragging match each morning over who stayed the latest in their office. Who is the most tired? Who clocked up the most hours? Who has sacrificed more of their life to the job? Is this really what success looks like these days? Do you really want that kind of badge of honour?

Right now, I am doubled over in pain from period cramps. It reminds me of a meme that says, 'Woman enjoys ten minutes where she is not premenstrual, on her period or post-menstrual!' I am feeling very sorry for myself, my stomach hurts and I know that I need to lie in bed rather than plough on with work. But I also know that if I don't just 'get on with it' I will feel bad, worried that I'm slipping behind. In any case, it's still easier to tell your boss you have cramps, so you won't be able to work, than to tell her about the days when your mood is so low that you can't focus properly. (I'm my own boss, and still have to remind myself to be understanding towards to my employees – including me!). In 2019, I wrote a piece for *The Times* about how research shows that we'd rather straight up lie and say we have tummy ache than be honest and say we need a duvet day or mental health day. There is still so much stigma, and it's harder to admit things (to ourselves and others), then communicate the complexities of our mind, and also work out what we need to make us feel better. There is a collective sense of needing to soldier on and not be seen as 'weak', which is of course not the truth. The comments on the *Times* article were mixed, and while some people agreed we need to be more honest about mental health, others said that I wouldn't have lasted long at their company and that they would have given me a P45. In their heads, the correct headline would read: 'Entitled millennial takes time off for her mental health'. We are still working out how to talk about mental health at work, and how we can show that it is not a sign of weakness in a system that wants us never to stop working, but actually a strength to be able to lift it out of the shadows and talk openly about it.

Someone I know who runs a large company confessed that he found his Gen Z employees 'difficult to manage' because they request to take mental health days off work. I understand that businesses need to run smoothly, but I couldn't help but wonder why he wouldn't address the obvious elephant in the room: that surely examining the root cause of his employees' suffering would be a better long-term solution than just being annoyed that they were constantly crumbling? There is a problem with the workplace as it is. If we break, we are reprimanded. It's not sustainable. We have to start being curious about the statistics and ask ourselves why so many people find themselves unable to keep up with the ridiculous pace of modern work, especially when we have the technology that was supposed to help. Something isn't working.

Now I'm self-employed, I try and be a good boss to myself. On one of my self-imposed duvet days, I'm scrolling through Instagram and I see a quote from Will Smith, who says his secret to success is a 'sickening work ethic', while multiple posts flash by about 'putting in your ten thousand hours' (a method popularized by author Malcolm Gladwell in his book *Outliers: The Story of Success*) to learn a new skill. Then I see an advert for an app that claims to help you absorb the contents of forty self-help books in a week (forty!). Snippets of each book and the 'key takeaways' are narrated by a robotic voice. You can 'read' a whole Eckhart Tolle book in under ten minutes. It feels as though productive self-improvement has taken on a bro-culture vibe. It feels aggressive and intense, this quest to improve. These apps take the joy out of reading, plus, if you need to keep consuming more and more of them to get the answers, can any of these self-help books really claim to have the keys to happiness and success?

But it's no wonder there's an engaged market for this app when you can't get away from the increasing demands and questions such as 'Can you work under pressure?' in our modern work culture. It is a requirement for pretty much every job, not just those who are saving lives in A&E or in a fire station. Why should every job need to be high pressure?

We have bastardized the idea of what 'urgent' is. We can't get away from the message that only extremely high levels of 'success' will do, and to get there we need to hustle harder and longer, when actually we need a break from it all. We feel the constant pressure to be giving more.

Time's Up for Overtime

At a recent wedding, as my husband and I made our way to a large circular dining table draped with a tablecloth, with a beautiful flower laid delicately on each plate, we discovered that the bride and groom had mixed the seating plan up so guests could mingle. Fun for extroverts, not so much for introverts like me. I was sat next to a man in his mid-thirties who said he was a lawyer. He was polite, but he could hardly keep his eyes open. We got chatting a bit about work, which everyone seems to do at weddings to fill the awkward silences. He apologized for being so tired and unable to focus on the conversation much, and told me that the work-load was so crazy at his law firm that he'd been sleeping approximately three hours a night, and sometimes he even slept in the office in his clothes. When someone else at the table naively asked why lawyers don't share the workload, tag-team or work in shifts, he just laughed. 'No. That's not how it works.' One human being bears the individual end-less load and is responsible for all the work from their specific client. He looked *so* tired. All I could think was, what is the point in getting a sticker for being most productive when you are unable to enjoy other areas of your life and are too tired to function? What's the point in being so tired at social events that you might as well not bother going? Why is this state of exhaustion so normalized?

We are told that our jobs are meant to give us purpose, so it follows that working all hours of the day is for a greater good. We have been fed the idea that having a job isn't enough, we have to be passionate about it too. Many of us no longer leave work in the office; we actually take it along with us on holiday. Author Sam Baker made a good point in an article discussing burnout: 'The 1980s were, "Put on a suit and work till you drop",' she says. 'Mark Zuckerberg is, "Put on a grey T-shirt and work till you drop".' The difference, she says, is that 'it's all now cloaked in a higher mission'. This obsession with meaning, 'passion' and purpose is just a smokescreen to keep us all working harder. No matter its worth to society, output is the holy grail. But I think it is a scam, especially if you are working for a big faceless com-pany that would replace you in a heartbeat. We are supposed to care about our jobs in a climate where employers don't seem to care about us.

In my 2018 book *The Multi-Hyphen Method*, I also point out that the advancement and evolution of technology should mean that we don't need to sit on the same chair for a rigid eight-hour stint: a shift pattern invented during the Industrial Revolution to make the most of daylight hours. It's ridiculously outdated. Extremely labour-intensive work is now helped along by machines, but instead of this letting humans work differently, people are still trapped by the system of endless working hours, even if that job adds no real value to society. It's productivity for productivity's sake. You might have heard the phrase 'bullshit jobs', a term coined by anthropologist David Graeber, who was a professor at the London School of Economics. He argued that there are millions of people slogging away at jobs which contribute very little to society, and they know it. Sending emails back and forth about pointless, non-urgent things that are treated as if they are urgent. People go to bed at night not really knowing what they are doing, if their job really means anything, or if they are just going back and forth over emails all day long for the sake of it. During the pandemic, many of us had to face the reality that many of our jobs were indeed 'non-essential'.

Post-pandemic, while companies are starting to address these issues, looking at a more flexible working culture, productivity still seems to be the end goal for most of them.

These necessary new ways of working are simply a matter of fairness and improve wellbeing, yet in our capitalistic culture they still have to be justified in terms of productivity and revenue. Does it directly impact the bottom line? Well then, we might consider it! The proposals for the four-day week are all based around productivity. The arguments for working from home all revolve around increasing productivity. It feels very strange, in an increasingly technological world, to treat humans as pieces of machinery. Everything seems to come back to money, and our health and freedoms are suffering because of it.

Many of us *want* to care about our jobs, but we don't want to be treated unfairly by top bosses who demand we are passionate. No one wants to be passionate on command, if such a thing is even possible; we want to feel an element of freedom, independence and excitement when it comes to our passions. Working with ridiculous demands upon us can make us resentful. There is such a thing as 'revenge bedtime procrastination', which emerged from a Chinese expression about the frustration we feel when overwork and stressful hours leave hardly any time for leisure. Revenge bedtime procrastination is the act of sacrificing our sleep for the leisure time we so desperately want. So, you might be pottering about refusing to go to bed, or you will lie in bed, your eyes aching with tiredness and read, scroll, watch Netflix, or do anything to squeeze more time out of the day. The Sleep Foundation says: 'For people in high-stress jobs that take up the bulk of their day, revenge bedtime procrastination is a way to find a few hours of entertainment even though it results in insufficient sleep.' The idea of working so many hours that you end up harming yourself even more by seeking leisure time 'revenge' seems wild to me. On speaking to an acquaintance who works really long hours in the property industry on commission, she admitted to something I will call 'retail therapy revenge': spending loads of her money on pointless stuff just to feel like the job she hated was worth it. There's an irony here: in spending so much of her income on stuff she didn't need or like, she probably ended up with the same amount in her account as if she worked fewer hours in a job that would give her more happiness and freedom. The money itself was not making her any happier, it was just being used as a means to an end and a distraction from looking at the truth (something I'll explore more in the Money Myth chapter).

One benefit of being a founder or a business owner is that you lay down the ground rules and can employ people you feel you can be honest with. With my team, I can be absolutely open if I'm struggling mentally or feel burnt out, and they know they can open up to me too. If we normalize the conversation, when we hear the words 'mental health', we understand it is just as important as physical health. It is technically physical too: mental health is also brain health. As the author Elizabeth Gilbert put it on an episode of my podcast: each day 'we have a different weather forecast in our minds'. Some days are sunny, and some days are stormy. We are not machines and cannot be expected to simply flip a switch to set our internal programming to perform at the same default level every day. We can only truly feel successful when we stop acting like robots that can be optimized, and embrace the fact we are human.

Productivity Shame

It's been hard to shift my feelings of shame around productivity, or a lack of it, though. For many of us, our relationship with our output in life is so deeply ingrained. My relationship with productivity has swung around almost 180 degrees. In my twenties, I would see resting as shameful so I was constantly busy; now, ten years later, I see workaholism as shameful and that I *shouldn't* be so busy. Whatever way I look at it, I have to check in with myself and stop shaming myself. As I said in the first chapter, the idea of perfect 'balance' is also a myth. I don't want to be embarrassed about my intense stints of productivity, or ashamed of them. And I don't want to be embarrassed by or ashamed of the fact that I now take August and December entirely off work to rest and travel, either. It's as though whatever way we slice it, we can always make ourselves feel like we're doing it wrong in someone else's eyes. This is why it's so important to trust yourself and make sure you are doing what feels right for you. We all have different limits, lives and goals.

My relationship with productivity has been an interesting one to uncover. Talking with friends, a therapist and a life coach revealed why I always had to be busy, and why I didn't feel worthy of rest. For me, it's a combination of schooling, my personality, my fears (and being a millennial, probably). Every generation has a complex relationship with work and rest, but millennials graduated into a recession; there was a very strong fear that you would be homeless and jobless if you didn't work extremely hard as jobs were limited, but I wonder whether some of us missed the memo that 'working hard' doesn't mean giving yourself a nervous breakdown. My first session with my life coach approached this head-on, and there was no messing around. When I spoke to her about my work, my career and my creativity, I used phrases like: 'I have to get on with it', 'I have to nail it down' and 'I'll make myself get on top of it'. The language was quite aggressive and unforgiving, as though I was using it as a stick to beat myself with. Clearly, I was someone who used to see breaks or rest or days off as weakness, and it was a long road to learning a different way. And many of my peers clearly felt the same.

Productivity til You Drop

Author Abigail Bergstrom wrote openly about her burnout experience, in a *Times* article in 2022. She explained that her old 'busy' life looked successful to the outside world, packed out with back-to-back meetings: 'In my old life every ticking minute was accounted for from the moment I opened my eyes. I'd combine a walk to the Tube with a client call, and a trip to get a bikini wax with an opportunity to order those Mother's Day flowers and book a table. Each action was multitasked, every half-hour slot blocked out in my diary.' Abigail had done everything 'right': she was productive, she had a busy diary, she was young, she was successful. And yet: she wasn't listening to the signs from her body, until one day it took over for her, and forced her to become bed-bound for months.

Burnout demands rest. The body gives us warning signs, and if we ignore them, then it forces us to stop. A good friend of mine's hands froze over her laptop one day: exhausted and unable to do much without crying or being overwhelmed, she was signed off work for three months because of burnout. She said she'd missed the warning signs, and then it felt too late. She was in bed, like Abigail, for months recovering. Another friend, who had a career in the NHS, quit to go travelling after spending the previous two years being forced into using skills and initiative well beyond her qualifications in intensive care units during the pandemic. She is currently sending me voice notes from the Galápagos Islands. Another friend worked so hard, her skin physically flared up, her face and neck swelling dangerously, and she said herself that if she hadn't had such physical symptoms forcing her to rest, she probably wouldn't have listened. Another has moved to Wales to 'rewild' her life: leaving the madness of New York, growing radishes in the garden, saying hello to the birds and running a start-up from home.

Everywhere you look, people are not OK. Burnt out. Stressed. At their limits. There seems to be a switch happening. We are no longer going to put up with risking our minds and bodies working for companies that don't even care if we leave anyway. We're discovering we're all replaceable, so it's a good time to work out what we actually want from our lives, should we need to pivot.

Are we all tired of the same old bullshit? Are the modern-day expectations placed upon us finally feeling out of kilter? Selina Barker, author of *Burnout*, thinks so. 'When we came out of the first lockdown here in the UK, other coaches and therapists I spoke to said they were seeing the same thing: a wonderful weariness that was making us either unwilling or simply incapable of putting up with the kind of bullshit we once thought we *had* to put up with. The bullshit of being treated like machines (by companies *and* by ourselves), the bullshit of toxic productivity, the bullshit of letting companies think that paying us means somehow owning us, the bullshit of life being an urgent race to keep up with a never-ending to-do list.' (I personally love how many times she said bullshit.)

Recently, thanks to TikTok, the trend of 'quiet quitting' went viral online. This doesn't mean actually leaving your job but quitting the endless insatiable need for doing more at work; it means clocking off dead on time, no sucking up to the boss, no emails in the evenings or weekends. Basically 'quiet quitting' means just doing your job as requested without overtime. Some people felt it was a great way to push back on productivity culture, but of course many people branded it 'lazy'. We're not yet free from the vice-like hold hustle culture has over us.

Letting Go of Our Obsession with 'Routines'

It's difficult for both men and women to let go of the productivity trap: men may feel they need to work harder in their traditional role as a 'provider', and many women have been made to feel like their purpose is being useful to others and to adhere to that annoying stereotype that we are good multi-taskers. As we saw with the idea around 'having it all', women are often made to feel guilty for not doing everything to the highest standard: working, parenting, nurturing.

It's no wonder we feel the pressure to be productive when so much of what we consume is feeding us this message that we should be doing more. Years back, I read a book called *I Don't Know How She Does It*, which was turned into a film starring Sarah Jessica Parker wearing expensive shoes. It dramatizes 'the dilemma of working motherhood at the start of the twenty-first century', and its title is a turn of phrase I now use to describe a certain type of interview very popular with the media. An 'I Don't Know How She Does It' interview (let's shorten to IDKHSDI for the sake of brevity) portrays a female interviewee as though she has solved the dilemma of having zero time and multiple plates to spin, while making life look so easy. You know the type: where the woman gets up at five a.m. and dresses her six perfect children, while sporting a perfect blow-dry, or where a prominent CEO admits, 'My assistant Penelope is in my inbox all day. We have a very elaborate colour-coding system for my inbox with over sixty categories of emails.' This appetite for IDKHSDI articles means other people's immaculate, envy-inducing routines are splashed all over the internet, making us believe they are realistic and inspirational, when really, they are just making us all panic that we're doing it wrong. It's a pyramid scheme of 'productivity advice'. It's like seeing the ballet shoe without glimpsing the ruined toes inside. It makes us feel small, like our way of doing things is probably wrong.

Culturally, we appear to be obsessed with successful people's routines. The subtext is: if only we, too, had a great routine, then we could also be successful. I've heard of many different bizarre routines ranging from having an orgasm before working to writing a bestselling novel in the bath in the mornings. It's a fun way to sell the idea of success to us, but I just don't buy it. Stephen King supposedly writes between eleven thirty a.m. and one thirty p.m. each day, but, by following his lead, that doesn't mean any of us would miraculously then be able to write a Stephen King novel. As mentioned in the earlier chapter about the success 'formula' myth: there are too many other factors at play.

I interviewed Madeline Dore, author of *I Didn't Do the Thing Today*, about her obsession with 'successful' people and their routines. She said, 'We want there to be a cure. We think: here's this thing that's going to make us more productive, more successful, richer, prettier, happier. And it seems so simple. If it's like: oh, if only I could get up at five a.m., all of my life's problems will be solved in that thing. So maybe that's the appeal of it. And because I'm telling myself that I'll only be happy and successful when I'm someone who gets up at five a.m., that's so easy to sabotage. And it means that I'm perpetually postponing my life, until I become this person. That might not be who I really want to be. Maybe getting up at five in the morning means that I am grumpy all day because I'm sleep deprived. And maybe that's actually causing far more harm than good.' She eventually came to realize that we are all different, and we should just lean into our own ways of doing things. A 'perfect' rigid routine is not the answer to success, it's actually the ability to be flexible, often.

Confession time: whenever I give an interview and the host asks me if I have 'a routine', I tell a white lie. Well, I tell them about a recent 'good day' because every day is different for me. I usually admit this, but I have probably added to the IDKHSDI pile at some point. On a 'good' day I wake up early, light a candle, have a healthy breakfast, do some stretches and then get down to four solid hours of great 'deep work' before going for a walk, having lunch, and then continuing on with my super-productive day before winding down and having some self-care time. But this is not my 'usual' routine! At all! This is the once-in-a-blue-moon day that goes well. I don't always get the greatest amount of work done on those days either. I just feel good because society and magazines have made me feel like I 'should' have a routine that I religiously stick to.

I have often been a bit embarrassed about my lack of routine. I've never had a regular one, and I probably never will. But they can be useful at times. The Covid pandemic felt like collective 'limbo', and it is normal to go through transitional periods of life when we just don't know what's going to happen. I will never be someone with a solid routine. But in these moments, I use something I call Temporary Routines. These are routines I have stocked and saved for when shit hits the fan in liminal moments of my life and I need some structure, but the rest of the time, I go with the disorderly flow of life.

My Temporary Routines are made up of certain rituals I've made a note of over the years. They are ready-made, proven behaviours (bespoke to me) that just seem to work when I need to feel grounded and settled. They include, in no particular order: a break from social media, practising author and creativity coach Julia Cameron's morning pages (three-pages of long-hand writing, which kickstarts my creativity and gets things off my chest), using a Pomodoro timer to help me write for twenty-five minutes at a time, and taking a thirty-minute lunchtime walk around my local park. I also incorporate three breaks that act as 'mind meals' into my day, which is something I learned from therapist Anna Mathur. Just as you feed yourself food three times a day, feed your brain too (take a walk, read a chapter of a book, preserve a moment to sit quietly). It is not about having an award-winning routine that you rigidly stick to every single day. Copying someone else's routine isn't what will make you successful at your own life, it's crafting your own that will help you stay afloat. It's about having various tools in your back pocket to help you get through a good, bad or average day. It's about saying, 'This is my routine for now,' or 'Let's try this.' Then, the routine goes out of the window again. Nothing is for ever. Everything is temporary. Routines can be useful, but they don't need to stick or stay. We can change them up whenever we want.

There can be magic in abandoning rigidity. Not only is it human nature to let things slide, be a bit messy, and let things move to their natural rhythms, but I get my best ideas when I'm least expecting them. As author Taffy Brodesser-Akner writes, 'Sometimes a little chaos gets things done.' Some of people's best ideas do not come from any sense of order or routine, just as productivity does not come from micro-managing every ounce of the day. Not everything has to turn into something productive either. Not everything has to be a routined side hustle. Great things can happen naturally, organically, for fun.

A Changed Outlook

The pandemic made many of us weary, grinding us down, and some of us were left with ongoing health issues. I do not have the same energy or capacity for endless work like I did before the pandemic. But thanks to my sessions with my life coach, I am more in tune with my body now. They taught me how to listen to my body (having a trained profes-sional take me through 'the body compass'), prioritize rest, quieten down negative self-talk and, crucially, let people see the real me. I realized I had been covering myself up with busyness, with my career. Underneath all of that: who was the real me? Who was I before I got sucked into the world of work? How do I get her back?

Now, when it feels wrong to be stressing myself and over-working, I do something about it. On Martha Beck and Rowan Mangan's podcast Bewildered, an episode called 'The

Productivity Addict' explains how we can work from a place of flow, instead of a place of stress. It's not about being unproductive but being productive in a better way. When we are being 'productive' from a place of stress, we are maxing out our adrenaline, and when we are being productive from a place of love, we are feeling the effects of oxytocin. This exercise they recommend below has saved me so many times when I've felt myself spinning slightly out of control:

1. Press your back up against a chair, or a wall (put gentle pressure on the body).

2. Put your arms around your ribcage like you are hugging yourself.

3. Breathe regularly and slowly, breathing out very slow on the exhales.

4. Look at everything in the room around you that is red, yellow or white.

Martha says the reason this calms your nervous system is because if we were pursued by a predator, our breathing and heart rate would go through the roof, signalling that we were in danger. By breathing slowly and calmly, you are telling your body that you are not in danger. You are OK. Now you can move leisurely through the day, even if you have lots to do, instead of stressing. Sounds good, doesn't it?

Stopping completely used to be an alien concept to me. In a world of passion projects, hobbies, the boundless opportunities of the internet, hybrid working and the constant sharing of our lives online, I found it difficult to pinpoint what it means to purely rest. Even when we are poorly we find it hard to slow down; most of us have worked through illness. According to a study conducted by Robert Half, 90 per cent of employees admit they have gone to work when sick. I was on a Zoom recently and someone started coughing non-stop, she then told me she had Covid. 'Why are you working?' I asked, begging her to go and lie down, but she insisted she didn't want to miss the meeting, and I had a feeling she was on a tight deadline for the very thing we were discussing. 'Everyone is working through Covid,' she replied. For so long we've normalized working through illness, we've normalized the eye-roll that colleagues give you when you need a doctor's appointment, and we've normalized dragging our disgusting snotty selves into the office, proving to others (and ourselves?) that we are invincible. We've normalized calling in sick only for our bosses to keep pestering us with urgent work. Flexible working has only made resting while unwell even harder, as our work can be taken to our sickbeds so easily.

You don't have to be a workplace martyr. We shouldn't have to work through illness. Bosses should be more understanding: more human, less machine. But then, bosses are stressed too, and the cycle continues. We simply can't be on form every single day for 365 days a year. It would be sheer lunacy to even try. Maybe we should be more like author and activist Nova Reid, whose out-of-office inspired me. 'I have undertaken an extraordinary 18 months ending with an incredible book tour for the launch of my debut book *The Good Ally*. I cannot thank you enough for your support and business during this time. I will now be doing the opposite of what society expects of Black women and resting – because white supremacy will be here when I get back. I am now on sabbatical until . . .' It's important to point out that Nova's work in the anti-racism space means she actively has to protect herself and her time, because showing up to do the work takes a huge mental and emotional toll. But we can all take a leaf from her book. She is someone I admire, for her strong and well carved-out boundaries.

We Need a Break . . . from Our Minds

But simply taking a break from work isn't going to cut it in our productivity-obsessed world. We need to change our idea of productivity altogether. A new coaching client of mine came to me with a problem: although she was exhausted, on her holidays all she could do was work, when really all she wanted was to enjoy her break, have some rest, do some yoga and have a big lie down. She described waking up with an 'agenda' each day. Everything, from her yoga to lying in a hammock, went on her to-do list, so even the way she spoke about rest sounded like it was a job to do. Yes, sure, she was lying on a beach somewhere hot, but she wasn't actually resting because she had so much pent-up stress and pressure inside her. She was treating the task of 'resting' like it was bootcamp.

We uncovered that this was stemming from something way back in her childhood: her parents never allowed her to rest growing up. When she would sit in the garden as a child to read a book and relax, it was yanked out of her hands and she was told to be useful, to get to work. Her early memories and lived experiences had bedded in, and she'd need to take time to unpick them. Sometimes our relationship with productivity is much deeper than just our preference for certain routines. Sometimes it runs incredibly deep indeed.

So many of us feel like everything has to be ticked off before we can stop, and if we're not being 'useful', we feel as though we will be punished by someone, even if just by ourselves. It's something to take seriously and it is worth investing in your own healing journey with support.

'I'm terrible at resting!' often comes across in conversation as a cute character quirk. But most of the time it's true – we are terrible at it, for many different reasons. We don't see rest as a 'skill', but it is a skill – and one that needs to be practised. According to Alex Soojung-Kim Pang (author of *Rest*), 'Rest is like breathing or running. On the one hand, it's completely natural; on the other hand, it's something you can learn to do better.' Some people claim we should make our rest 'better' in order to be more productive in the long run, but I want to take a stand against that. We need to find better ways to actually rest for rest's sake. For me, there's nothing worse than spending a 'rest' weekend secretly doing bits of work here and there, because I can't adjust to the boredom and quietness of it all.

Rest feels like an act of rebellion in a world that doesn't want us to stop. And if we don't know how to rest, it doesn't matter if we are in a hammock, a bare room or staring at an ocean view, we are going to feel exhausted when we go back to daily life. We need to embrace the fact that ease is the new hustle. We need to acknowledge that if something costs you your mental health, it is too expensive. You have a mind and body budget: a certain amount of currency that you're spending every day. We cannot sustain our 'always on' life-styles. Rest gives us many biological benefits: a healthier heart, sharper brain function, increased mood, better immunity (and tons more). The consequences of a lack of rest impact our health in the short- and long-term. We need to take it seriously individually, but also as a wider culture.

For a lot of us, we were praised as young children for how much we worked, and our hard work was seen as the value we brought to the world, so as adults we build a codependent relationship with productivity. The challenge now is to see our inherent value outside of what we produce in a capitalist world that wants to take, take, take. Things are changing: in Portugal it is now illegal for your boss to text you after work, a revolutionary remote-work law that acknowledges a version of success outside of work and helps workers to get their lives back. In France, there has been 'the right to disconnect' since 2016, which means employers cannot contact their employees outside of work hours.

Author and consultant Samantha Clarke opened my eyes recently to the fact that there are many different types of rest. Of course, there's physical rest, which we can achieve through breath work or relaxing the body. But there's also mental rest, which involves things like meditating or running; social rest, which you can get from seeing a good friend or having a nourishing phone call; and spiritual rest, achieved by practising gratitude. I have been consciously trying to factor more of these restful moments into my week, and I feel so much more in touch with myself and my most basic needs.

Setting Productivity Boundaries

It's only since my thirties that I've felt the inner confidence to settle into who I really am and be comfortable with putting boundaries around my energy. I just didn't feel brave enough to do it in my twenties; I still felt at the beck and call of other people. Of course, there are nuances around introversion and extroversion, and we are all on a sliding scale. But if we take the more general definition of being an introvert: I get energy from being on my own or with one other person, as opposed to getting energy from a bigger group or more sociable situation. After big work things, networking or events, I try to schedule in a recovery day. This is why, during my twenties, I loved living with my most extroverted friend. Doing things with her meant I could deflect some of the overwhelm. She would soak up all the energy in the room like a solar panel: she'd capture it and convert it into electricity for the both of us. She was powering herself from other people, whereas I would feel my battery drain, like a device bleeping dramatically that it only has 1 per cent left. We all have a finite amount of energy to give each day and that level is different for each of us. I recently learned about 'spoon theory', coined by Christine Miserandino, which is popular among many people dealing with chronic illness. She explains how each person has a different number of 'spoons' to give the world each day – we're not all alike. Author Simon Sinek uses the analogy of 'coins' to describe energy exchanges and how we each start the day with a different number of coins.

Creativity and writing are things that give me energy (or spoons or coins), as opposed to draining it. But this also means I can be prone to overworking, because I just don't know when to stop. Even if you love your work, when it morphs into escapism it can upset the scales, because you're suddenly out of sync with your body (I explore this delicate tension more in the 'You Are Your Job' Myth chapter later). When too much petrol is put in a car, it breaks, stops working, and it is very costly to repair. It's a balancing act of leaning into the things that give you spoons and knowing when to actively rest. I am lucky that I can design my own day. I work for myself and I don't have kids. And I believe that as long as employees aren't trusted or respected as individuals to work to their own bodily rhythms, the world of work will remain broken. Nine-to-five can be the least productive part of the day for some people, as it misses the dawn boost of the early-morning riser or the late-night wonder of the night owl. We each get surges of energy in different parts of the day, and only when we learn to regulate our own energy in a way that serves us can we really make magic happen.

Letting go of our desire to be productive is difficult, because for many of us it is so ingrained in the expectations we may have of ourselves and because we've been told that productivity equals success and therefore a meaningful life. Technology has helped us become more productive, but instead of kicking back and letting the tech and tools (i.e. robot vacuum cleaners) lighten the load, we use it to go and do even more work. One of the main ways we can learn to pay attention to our own addiction to productivity is by checking in with our bodies. When our heart is racing but we do nothing about it, or we are hungry yet skipping meals, pushing through when we need the loo, multitasking while telling ourselves we'll 'just do one more thing', it's time to look closely at our idea of productivity. We can have a warped view of our work if we don't take a step back.

The phrase 'productivity dysmorphia' was coined in 2021 by journalist and author Anna Codrea-Rado. In an article for Refinery 29, she described how, when she wrote a list of everything she'd done 'since the beginning of the pandemic', which consisted of a huge number of achievements including how she 'pitched and published a book, launched a media awards ceremony and hosted two podcasts', she felt 'over-whelmed'. She then wrote, 'The only thing more overwhelming is that I feel like I've done nothing at all.' The notion of simply not being able to take in, or register, how productive you've been because there's always more to do resonated with lots of readers. It captured the modern condition of being so productive that none of our achievements end up standing out or being savoured or celebrated. We just churn stuff out, feeling empty and hollow at the end of it. I asked Anna why she thinks her piece spoke to so many people. She said, 'I was trying to capture this feeling of not being able to see one's own success. So, being super-productive, and really pushing to do and achieve more, but then somehow not being able to enjoy the fruits of that productivity.' The more productive we are, the more we risk detaching ourselves from the outcomes, making us unable to acknowledge our success. We need to look at celebrating our wins along the way, and perhaps have fewer goals to focus on, instead of staring down the barrel of a long, overwhelming list. When we achieve too much, essentially we start becoming numb to it.

Productivity for productivity's sake never feels good, because it's a never-ending game of more, more, more. Rather than chasing productivity, there's another way to measure our progress, and that's to acknowledge our success. A friend of mine keeps a 'success diary', just for her, that logs all of the small (and big) wins along the way, so that she can remind herself how far she's come. It's no good doing it at the end of the process, you need to be able to celebrate what you're doing in the moment.

Sometimes, we use 'busyness' as a distraction from making a big decision about our lives. We cover up our feelings with our work, with our diary, with other people's needs. In my coaching sessions, I find most people are putting off something out of fear. Why would they bother writing a book, or training for a marathon, or launching a business if there's a chance they might fail? They fill their time with less important, endless tasks, rather than focusing on the goals that matter. Having a goal we care about is scary. So how do we get around this block?

Milestone Goals vs Process Goals

The question I come back to is this: is it really success in the end if you had a miserable time getting there? Recently I have been much more curious about enjoying the process of something rather than jumping straight to my daydreams of a fantasy outcome. Since I discovered the difference between 'process goals' and 'milestone goals', everything has changed.

With a milestone goal, it's all about the end achievement, like running a marathon, whereas a process goal could be 'training for a marathon' or even 'enjoy training for a marathon'. The process goal is not just about the goal itself but about experiencing it, being present for it, noticing the time spent on it and learning to congratulate yourself along the way. I've been focusing on process goals for a while, trying to make sure I enjoy (in whatever way I can) the writing of my books, not just the moments when they publish. Otherwise, the final 'goal' and feeling I'd been waiting to get would feel like an anticlimax, regardless of how well I did. Most of our lives are spent 'doing' rather than 'achieving', so we might as well enjoy the process.

Here are some examples of milestone goals vs process goals:

- Instead of 'I'm going to write a book' (milestone goal), you focus on 'I'm going to write for twenty minutes a day' (process goal).
- Instead of 'I'm going to beat last year's reading goal' (milestone goal), you focus on 'I'm going to read for half an hour every Sunday' (process goal).
- Instead of 'I'm going to win an Oscar' (milestone goal), how can you find enjoyment in the smaller day-to-day moments of film-making?

- Instead of 'I'm going to get really fit' (milestone goal), you focus on 'I'm going to enjoy an at-home workout three mornings a week' (process goal).

As an added bonus, enjoying the process can also lead to more success, because we show up more committed, motivated and in a state of flow. Psychologist Emma Hepburn agrees: 'There's lots of good evidence that we are more likely to enjoy and achieve our goals if we can focus on the process and enjoy this, rather than being focused solely on the end goal. For example, with exercise, this could mean enjoying the after-effects of how it made me feel, rather than trying to obtain a weight goal. With a job it's connecting to the parts that are important to you, rather than seeing that you need to constantly strive for a promotion. Abandoning the idea of getting to the mythical "there" is ultimately helpful, as you can shift your focus to connecting to your "why" in the here and now rather than waiting for something that won't actually bring what you hope for.'

Constant productivity is forced on us by our capitalist culture and workplaces. It's so ingrained in our society that many retired workers still find themselves constantly busying themselves because they don't know any other way. If we have been told since childhood to always be working, doing, making ourselves useful for the sake of it, it's no wonder we don't know how to enjoy rest. But being constantly busy won't make us more useful; it only leads to stress, poor mental and physical health, and burnout. As a society, we need to embrace the art of rest, and as individuals we can start to set better boundaries and see our value outside of our output. Only then can we truly enjoy the process of achieving our goals.

Chapter Reflections

1. **What would compassion for yourself look like, on a day you feel you can't be productive?** It is human nature to want to create, to thrive, to do things. But sometimes our bodies are telling us we need to slow down. What compassionate words of wisdom could you tell yourself when you are in need of rest? For me it's something like this: 'You deserve to rest without question or reason.'

2. **What productivity pressures are you putting on yourself?** How do you treat yourself and others when you feel constantly caught up in productivity? Can you reduce your to-do list?

What advice would you give to a friend struggling in your position? Could productivity mean getting the urgent things done, and not putting too much on your plate? Write a new to-do list and move any deadlines you can, or ask for more time. Experiment with doing more on your own terms instead.

3. **What feeling are you chasing when being productive (or having been productive)?** This will help you work out whether it's really a state of productivity that will give you that feeling, or if, in fact, there's another way to generate it. Do you believe that productivity will make you feel 'enough'? Are you looking for satisfaction? Are you wanting to feel settled? Are you trying to prove something to yourself? Are there some other ways to make yourself feel better, in your body?

4. **What does a proper mental well-being break look like to you?** There is the famous Confucius quote, 'Wherever you go, there you are.' Even by going on holiday we cannot escape our own minds and the stressful thoughts – so how can you incorporate mini brain-breaks into your day?

Could you read a page of a book, sit quietly or have a nap? What do smaller moments of rest look like to you?

5. **Does a routine help or hinder you?** It is OK to not have a routine, or to have a very simple one. How is your ideal day best spent? Make sure you build in breaks.

6. **Check in with your body.** Our bodies store so much rich information on how we feel, what we can accomplish, what is right for us. Whenever you start to feel panicked, caught in a loop, or completely terrified once you've agreed to do something in a record number of days, check in with yourself and your body and see if you can adjust anything (*see* point 2). If you can cancel, then do so.

FOUR

The 'You Are Your Job' Myth

Gymnastics is what you do. It's not who you are.

@DOMINQUE MOCEANU,
IN RESPONSE TO @SIMONE_BILES

One afternoon, a few years ago, I found myself with sweaty palms because a massage therapist asked me if I had any hobbies. She was gripping a clipboard which held the consultation form about 'my lifestyle' that I had just filled in. I had left the 'hobbies' section blank. 'You must do *something* for fun? Even something small?' she probed. It's not that I thought everyone should always have an array of ambitious hobbies, but surely I should have been able to think of *one thing* I currently did outside of work, for fun and enjoyment.

When was the last time I had been to a festival? A gig? Or had gone to the cinema on my own? Or for a swim? My 'hobbies' were non-existent, and it just highlighted there and then how my entire existence was work-related. It was a stark realization that I had nothing else going on and I burst into tears. That was the moment I started to accept that something needed to change, instead of constantly pretending everything was fine.

When I first heard the phrase 'you are not your job', I felt defensive. I pushed back on it. For some of us, our jobs *are* the main way we spend our time. Surely, to some extent, we *are* our jobs. We spend so much time at work. It's a huge part of who we are. I felt that because my job allowed me to be creative, then it must be OK for it to make up a big part of my personality. I love books, I love writing, I love interviewing: it's who I am. But the brilliant Toni Morrison quote – 'You are not the work you do; you are the person you are' – got me thinking. It's hard to deny it once you hear someone you admire say it. I realized that the more I conflated my personality with my job, the more unhappy I became. The more I branded myself as a 'writer' first, and led with my work over and above anything else, the further I felt from my core self. I am a person first, outside of the things I 'do'.

It's no wonder so many of us feel so personally caught up with our jobs. When I worked at a social media agency, I noticed they would often use the phrase 'work family' and often gave away perks to deter workers from ever leaving. I would be gifted free work trips, where we would drink beer and play games, and, at first, it seemed like fun. I was in my twenties and mucked in. But I hadn't spotted these were red flags, and it soon became clear that you were seen as more of a 'team player' if you were single and didn't really have a home life. Early on in your career in particular, it is easy to get sucked in to feeling like your whole self-worth is tied to what you are achieving, the accolades you are amassing and the 'cool' job you have. You can let the other parts of your life fall by the wayside; you end up not knowing what you do for fun.

Feeling like our jobs are a reflection of 'who we are' is often a trap. A job is a way of making money and, therefore, it can never reflect who you truly are, not really. It's almost impossible to be authentically *you* and earn a living. There is a pervasive narrative telling us we need to follow our dreams, to make our careers reflect who we really are. The pressure to do a job that brings status *and* money *and* fulfils your self-worth is pushing people into financial precarity. It is possible, but it's not easy – and, back to Chapter One, there's a whole host of elements at play, such as luck and timing too. There's no shame in finding a job that pays the bills and doesn't need to 'represent' us. If your full-time job isn't the thing that brings you the most joy, it doesn't make you a failure. Our jobs don't need to be an extension of ourselves if we don't want them to be. And even if you do earn money from something you enjoy, not even a Hollywood actor earns all their money solely from their passion – they sign sponsorship deals, or take on a lucrative role in a blockbuster, which gives them the freedom to work on more meaningful projects for less money. In Stanley Tucci's book *Taste*, he tells the story of how Edward G. Robinson, a Romanian-American actor during Hollywood's golden age, took on three films a year: one for money, one for love and one for the location. We all make strategic decisions and it's different for everybody. This is why I'm a fan of the Multi-Hyphen Method too, taking on different jobs for varying reasons can bring in different income streams and make up a bigger pie.

Through exploring the reasons why work often becomes our identity, we can find ways to separate our sense of self from our jobs. We need to peel back a layer to realize who we are deep down, and find a way of working that allows this to shine and be OK with the decisions we make.

A New Kind of Work Identity

We've all heard the saying, 'On your deathbed, you won't be wishing you spent more time in the office.' We all know this is true in many ways, but we can't seem to untangle ourselves from it, and work trickles into so many elements of our lives without us noticing. Untangling ourselves from our work selves is quite the task, because work makes up such a large, and important, proportion of our lives. Even though our relationship with work can never completely fulfil us, it's still an important interconnection that deserves analysis.

Work has changed, and we've not been able to keep up with it. We were brought up to follow one career path with one outcome. But the job-for-life doesn't exist any more, and the idea of a five-year plan seems outdated when we don't even know what the world will look like in five years' time. It feels so far removed now to think of the world in which my grandpa worked, for example. He stayed at the same company for his whole life, with his job security, work perks, and his feeling that he was really part of something for good, not having to worry about 'innovating' or 'pivoting' to constantly keep up with everything every five minutes. He could just get on with the job he was paid to do. But now companies are changing, growing or declining at breakneck speed, and organizations that we thought would be around for ever are no longer here.

So where do young people discover their employment in such a precarious, fast-changing world? Many young people find that using their identity is the best way of earning an income. As columnist Eva Wiseman recently wrote: 'Influencers, entrepreneurs, people whose bedrooms are also their office, Depop shop, yoga studio and bathbomb empire – these are not just creative people taking control of their lives, often these are also people who were born too late to find security or peace in traditional industries or workplaces, and so, in order to make their lives work, have been forced to make their lives their work, their careers their entire identity.' Although, as we've seen earlier in the book, the internet has levelled the playing field, many of us are forced to make our identity our work, because we don't feel we have the security of anything else. Jobs are no longer for life, employers no longer protect our livelihoods, or house people, so we work with what we've got – ourselves and the internet – and in some cases feel forced into monetizing our identity or creating a personal brand. We see it work for other people, so who can blame the TikTok stars or the *Love Island* wannabes, when the world isn't set up to allow us basic securities? When there is an element of survival mode, we try and build security however we can. It's not that young people *want* their jobs to be their lives, it's that they potentially don't have a lot of choice. This means it's also up to us to find some distance between the two, so that we don't end up working 24/7.

Survival mode often blurs the boundaries between work and life. This erasure is only made worse by the fact that being obsessive about work is one of the few socially acceptable addictions. Nobody will tell you to stop. We are still praised for piling more and more work on to our plates, and spending late nights in the office, even if it is quite obviously making us ill. With work, I could always roll up my sleeves and find a way to disappear into it, like taking some kind of socially acceptable drug.

Sometimes we do become our jobs and only then do we realize how toxic that can become and how much it takes from us. In my case, the hustle became entrenched because I was often selling *myself* as the product. When I went freelance, I built a digital platform to promote the best parts of me, using all the tools I'd learned as a social media editor for some of the world's largest brands. Cultivating 'a personal brand' was a big part of building my 'success'. But even though I am not a 'celebrity', I found making myself into a sellable entity online quite exhilarating at first, then, later on, dehumanizing. By tying my self-worth to work, I was putting a commercial value on myself and my purpose as a human being. I'd reduced myself to a product to be sold, abandoning myself and my true nature. You pull your 'best bits' to the front and hide anything unpalatable. You wear colours that catch people's eye in their feed. You need to be a commodity and can't care about selling out – it's the name of the game. And I know I'm not alone. In a recent interview on Steven Bartlett's *Diary of a CEO* podcast, Mary Portas talked about how she changed her hair back to its natural colour because people started to see her as just 'the orange bob' that she was famous for. She spoke of the loneliness that comes with being a walking parody of yourself, how the 'personal brand' can begin to feel like a performance where people no longer see the real *you* behind your business avatar. We are waking up to the idea that living our lives as a 'human brand' is probably not great for the psyche.

Human First

Being treated as a human being first and foremost is crucial to our wellbeing, but there are many instances when people are still not treated with respect. A 2021 study in *Frontiers in Psychology* looked into 'objectification in the workplace', which refers to the treatment of employees as 'workers' and not people. They studied 'dehumanization indicators' and ways in which workers were devalued and looked upon as objects – for example, an employee only acknowledged for their use or skill, an employee reduced to appearance only, or an employee treated as though they have no thoughts or emotions. They found that the consequences of objectification led to more occupational burnout, decrease of job satisfaction and depression. No surprises there.

Dehumanization occurs when someone becomes successful too. Even though you have many perks and privileges, you are still being seen as a worker first, a person second. The more successful you become, the more people treat you like public property. As Caroline O'Donoghue said in the *Irish Examiner*, in conversation with her friend and author Dolly Alderton, '[. . .] when you do something and it's successful, everyone in your life wants you to do your best to make it even more successful. They put you up for more events, more interviews, more public appearances, more magazine covers. And you think by agreeing to do this stuff you're just doing your job, but the whole time, you're flooding the market to the point where people don't see you as a person.' When someone becomes successful, they are turned into a commodity which can be milked to the point of burnout or emotional damage. If you don't set boundaries, you are at risk of being taken advantage of and ending up in situations you don't really want to be in.

But this isn't something we can just blame our bosses or the people around us for. Sometimes it is how we label ourselves, and we can trap ourselves within our own work narrative. As Arthur C. Brookes wrote in his piece 'You Are Not Your Work', 'I know many people who talk of almost nothing besides their work; who are saying, essentially, "I am my job." This may feel more humanizing and empowering than saying "I am my boss's tool," but that reasoning has a fatal flaw: In theory, you can ditch your boss and get a new job. You can't ditch *you*.' Thinking you *are* your job could mean you enter into a never-ending cycle of working harder and harder to validate your self-worth, losing sight of who you really are. You become a version of yourself that is for profit and not for joy. Defining yourself by your work is, no matter how you slice it, leading you away from the truth that your value relies on nothing other than your humanity.

Reframing Impostor Syndrome

Doing something that takes us away from our inner human nature can lead to impostor syndrome, because we aren't being ourselves. We don't have impostor syndrome while throwing a birthday party for a family member, or while running a bath or eating a hamburger. These are just things we do. When we are putting ourselves out there, performing in some way, or doing our jobs, it's hard not to feel like an impostor, because such things are not strictly natural. Because, deep down, we are not our jobs, so we are impostors to a certain extent. Personally, I don't love it being described as a 'syndrome'. A *Harvard Business Review* article points out that impostor syndrome 'is a diagnosis often given to women. But the fact that it's considered a *diagnosis* at all is problematic.'

It's only natural to feel a bit *un*natural sitting politely on a panel using our best 'speaking voice', or working at a desk all day with no natural lighting, or writing advertising for a toothpaste brand. They are all performances in a capitalist culture, and therefore as human beings we might feel like they aren't very 'us'. There are moments, of course, where we can feel aligned to our work, and it's useful to notice when those times are, compared with when we feel most impostor-like. For example, while helping a junior colleague, or public speaking, or offering creative solutions, there might be moments when you feel like this is your natural strength, a skill that you also enjoy, because you are genuinely connecting with something. But work is work, and it is impossible to feed our soul at all times while making money.

We feel like an impostor if the image we're projecting to the outside world is incongruent with our straight-up reality. We are witness to the ins and the outs of our own work that no one else sees. *You* see my finished, edited book; *I* see the shittiest of first drafts. But at moments like this, I always recall a great piece of advice from my dad: a little bit of doubt is always good. A little bit of doubt before handing in some important work makes me read it again. A little bit of doubt before crossing the road makes me look twice. A little bit of self-doubt prompts me to check in with a friend. We don't need to 'overcome' our impostor syndrome. There's no need to be battling with our emotions or feelings. Instead, we can lean into them and hold space for them, by talking them out or writing them down. We need to buy into our *own* brand of confidence or success. Confidence doesn't have to be loud and dominant; it could mean moving calmly and gently through your decisions, knowing that they make sense to you. There's a gentler way forward than always trying to *beat* stuff. If we conduct ourselves with more integrity and authenticity, we can lessen the sense of being an impostor.

Being a bit unsure, or having a little doubt, doesn't need to be pathologized. Doubt isn't bad, but when impostor syndrome takes over it can turn into a form of self-sabotage, beating ourselves up for being human. But there is a way to reframe it. You're likely to feel like an impostor if you never feel like you've 'mastered' your trade, but on the flip side you'll always be learning and growing. We will never 'master' anything fully. As author and marketeer Seth Godin has said in the past, 'Yes, you're an impostor. So am I and so is everyone else. We're all impostors. Everyone who is doing important work is working on something that might not work.' I love this way of looking at it. If you think you're an impostor, it probably means you're working on something exciting, new and fresh. You could be launching a new business, becoming a parent, or moving into an exciting new role. It's understandable that you might be doubting it or yourself when something means a lot to you and you haven't completely figured it out yet. Think of your identity as an explorer, rather than an impostor. Or think of it this way: you may feel impostor syndrome in an ever-evolving jobs market, but you can never be an impostor at being you.

Myth: Your Identity Is Set in Stone for Ever

Thinking you *are* your job when it's going well is one thing, but what about when you lose interest, or change what you're into, or lose your job completely? I would get defensive about my overworking tendencies because I knew my work identity, and all the hours I put into it, were built on shaky ground. Any identity built around the things you produce is not a secure foundation. I felt trapped in my role of 'high achiever' so was using work as a protective measure against the world, trying to boost my self-worth. It's well documented by life coaches and psychologists that when we chase success or money or fame, or whatever it is, we are actually chasing a feeling. I was wanting a feeling of contentment, of self-worth, of peace. Of 'having enough'. Feeling enough. It all boils down to the same thing each time. Clinging on to my work identity was a cover-up, a distraction, a way of not doing more work on my (actual) self.

And what happens when work doesn't give you the comfort you want it to? I spoke to Rebecca Seal, author of *SOLO*, who elaborated on the fact that grasping too tightly to your work identity means that you can be more wounded when things don't work out. She spoke about how you are confusing your self-worth with an element of your life that you can't actually control: 'Having one part of your identity be all-important makes it much harder when something goes wrong. If you ARE a writer/accountant/lecturer, above all else, what happens when you mess that role up, as we all will occasionally do? The emotional fallout can be much greater if we've given excess weight to a specific part of our identity.' Rebecca found that when she failed at something work-related, instead of being momentarily knocked back, she would take it as a huge personal failure. So now, she explains that her identity 'is more evenly spread around the different facets of my life, I take things going wrong both less seriously, and less personally'. I wonder if this is the crux of it: if we take the results of 'success' or 'failure' in our life less personally, we might live a happier, less stressed existence. Rebecca went on, 'I just object, almost morally, to the idea that our work output is the best thing about us. That we should prioritize earning and making and doing over the rest of the beauty that life has to offer, just because the late-capitalist system that we exist within demands that of us: earn spend earn spend earn spend. Of course, we all have to earn a living, but when did it become OK to behave as though work is absolutely the biggest and best part of ourselves? It's just work.' This is still uncomfortable for me to hear sometimes, even though deep down I know it's true. I love my work, my work does feel important to me, but she's right that it can't be the best thing about me. It's not. That's the challenge: realizing that there are good things about you that aren't contingent on someone praising them, validating them or giving you a gold star. It's just work.

When I asked her about her work identity, author and broadcaster Genelle Aldred said, 'The downside to putting so much importance on work, especially if it's out of your control, is it can be taken away and then who are you? And that's an existential crisis that you don't want to have every time something changes.' Even Harry Styles in a recent Zane Lowe interview articulates that 'Working is not everything about who I am, it's something I do. For a really long time I didn't really know who I was if I didn't [sing and perform] – and it's really scary – cos if this ends, am I going to be good at handling it? [. . .] I no longer feel like my overall happiness is dependent [on] whether a song goes here [gesturing low] or here [gesturing high].'

It is an interesting exercise to sit with yourself, to take away your work, and ask yourself, *Who am I underneath it all?* When we wrap ourselves up so tightly in our work, we are in danger of losing important parts of ourselves. I found that in my workaholic years I lost the fun side of myself, the silly side. I would look through photos and not find any of me smiling or laughing. I realized I hadn't belly-laughed for a while because I was too busy focusing on my goals and how stressed I was. There is so much joy to be found outside of our clambering need for success.

Psychologist Emma Hepburn, whose wonderful book *A Toolkit for Modern Life* has helped me through many wobbles, says, 'It's important to think about how you create balance in a way that makes your work sustainable *and* builds your identity outside work.' I use the 'hat' technique, in that I make sure I am aware of which 'hat' I am wearing at any particular time. I use this as a multi-hyphenate, wearing many hats over the course of a day or a week. Being a multi-hyphenate is not about multitasking. It's about having many different parts of your life from which you can build a balanced identity, not just putting all your worth into one kind of work, or one way of living. I used to want to merge absolutely everything, but I have realized I can be a whole person living with integrity *and* still ring-fence and categorize different parts of myself. I can also accept my different sides and allow them in. As I work from home, I have to create boundaries, so that my work and home life don't merge completely under one roof. I do this by working in an office room with a door that I close at the end of every day. It's important for me to switch between roles in a healthy way, especially as I often coach people, which means I have to be in a state of mind that is very focused and present for the client. In that moment, my identity is as a coach. But later that day, I might be on stage, and my writer-performer self will come out. I am accepting now of all these different parts of myself, knowing that, overall, I am a whole person who also makes mistakes and contradicts herself sometimes. I am not one thing; I am lots of things. I can work with all my different sides, by being aware of them and being OK with them all.

More broadly, I also use my 'work' and 'home' hats. If I am wearing my work hat, I'm fully focused on that, and once I'm wearing my home hat, I switch off from work. This also helps me work more flexibly. If I took some of Tuesday off, I might need to pop my work hat back on on a

Saturday to finish off anything outstanding. I have separate phones for work and personal use, and also use separate Instagram accounts. Do whatever you need to do to compartmentalize your life. You can't wear multiple hats at once. (You'll overheat.)

It's hard to feel like you are anything other than your job sometimes, in a world that makes you feel like your output is the reason you exist. There are many ways to separate out our different selves, and we should enjoy leaning into these different sides of ourselves. It is a good feeling when all our different sides can work together harmoniously too – we all have varying parts, but they make up one whole. When all our parts are given attention, we can feel as though we are being our one true self, in touch with our overall integrity as a complete person. Maybe this is what balance feels like.

Chapter Reflections

I. **Describe who you are outside of work.** Write a list of descriptors that has nothing to do with working, earning money or achieving anything. For example: I'm Emma, I'm a daughter, sister, wife and an auntie; I like wearing loud clothes, eighties' music, sitting in the garden, looking after my neighbour's dogs and drinking hot chocolate. How does this reflection make you feel?

2. **How would you define your work 'self'?**
Acknowledge and accept this part of yourself. You probably show up slightly differently at work, and that's OK. Think of an object you could use to enable you to switch into your work mode – for example, I wear a thick pair of glasses whenever I am on stage talking about my work; it helps me connect with this version of myself. At home, I wear lighter glasses. Both sides of me are 'authentic', just different.

3. **Which parts of your work make you feel most like an 'impostor'?** We all get moments of doubt, so take time to reflect on whether you feel like an impostor because you're trying something new, or whether it's because it doesn't feel very aligned to who you are. If you're trying something new, even if you feel wobbly, that's an exciting place to be. And if you feel impostor-ish because the task doesn't feel very true to who you are, what small steps can you take to sync it to your values? What tweaks can you make, what can you change, who can you speak to?

4. **Create more boundaries between work and home.** These can be psychological boundaries, such as listening to different music when working on a paid project versus a personal project, or physical boundaries like closing the door on your work at the end of the day. Communicate openly about your availability; try not to leave any openings (for example, don't include 'call me if urgent' on your out-of-office if you can help it). Let your family and friends know you don't want to talk about work on your next holiday. Identify different ways that help you switch off and communicate openly and honestly with your loved ones.

FIVE

The Celebrity Myth

'I was curled up, uncontrollably crying. Why should I be crying? Because from the outside, I'm OK. I've had an amazing football career, I'm now working on TV, I can still pay my bills, who am I to be sad? I've got everything going for me, right?'

ALEX SCOTT, *DIARY OF A CEO WITH*

STEVEN BARTLETT

At the 2016 Golden Globe Awards, Jim Carrey declared on stage, 'I'm two-time Golden Globe winner Jim Carrey. When I go to sleep, I dream about being *three-time* Golden Globe winner Jim Carrey – because then . . . I would be enough.' In classic Carrey style, his delivery is hilarious. And what's funnier is the reaction of the audience of Very Successful People, nervously laughing as they're faced with the fact that the *next thing* they win probably won't solve their problems either.

Even though not everyone wants to be a celebrity, all of us can fall into the trap of wanting status. The word 'celebrity' comes from the Latin *celebritas*, like celebration and renown, which has positive connotations. The Latin word *fama* is more about fame, reputation, rumour and news. Fewer people want the fame part, the rumours and the intrusive cycle of appearing in the news, but celebrity, this idea of being celebrated by the masses, appeals to the part of us that wants outside validation. According to *Columbia* magazine, 'People who sought fame in classical and medieval times wanted to be remembered after their deaths. The goal of modern celebrity is to be renowned during one's lifetime.' Nowadays, the cherry on top is to be a 'national treasure' or 'household name'. But whether we reach those lofty heights or not, being known and appreciated for what we do on this planet appeals to lots of people. We want recognition, in whatever way that manifests for each of us.

Fame is still a goal for many young people – and for people of any age. However, celebrities who are supposed to have all the elements of 'happiness' – endless money, security and recognition – often still talk about being unhappy. Why do we continue to think that being adored on the world's stage is synonymous with ultimate success and 'happy ever after'?

Why do we the public, and the media, treat celebrities in the dehumanizing way we do? Why do we assume their lives must be so much better and less stressful than ours? During my short time working on women's magazines, I was once prompted by my editor to find out if a female actress was secretly pregnant, instead of asking her how she puts her talent into making films that entertain and touch viewers across the world. It was the nature of the job: celebrities were products to be sold, and still are. We feel entitled to know their every move, because they have fame and money.

From this angle, and from my experiences of getting up close to it during certain points of my magazine career, fame doesn't look like something to aspire to when it can so easily turn into yet another way to be trapped.

It's human nature to want to be seen and validated. Fame, the desire to be celebrated and chasing applause is often called 'ego addiction'. It sounds negative, but isn't necessarily bad, just a part of living in a society that rewards people who have status. In psychoanalytic study, our ego is the part of our psyche that is conscious, responsible for our narrative of selfhood, and this part interacts the most closely with our external reality. When we want to be famous, we are often massaging our ego, whereas being of service or making a difference is less ego-led and more about the process of adding collective meaning. Romanticizing the idea of being famous for fame's sake has been exacerbated by social media, as followers are the new way of showing status. Studies have loosely suggested that insecure self-esteem can lead to a desire for fame, but as we'll see, it's not the fix we're hoping for.

As author of *The Status Game*, Will Storr told me, 'Status is deeply implicated in our desire for success. In fact, it's really one and the same thing. We've evolved to crave status – which is the feeling of being valued by other people – because we're a tribal animal. Back when our brains were evolving, when we proved ourselves valuable to the tribe, we rose in status – people thought better of us – and this led to important rewards, such as better access to food, safer sleeping sites, greater influence, greater access to our choice of mates.' It makes so much sense, then, that we crave status, as it has a direct correlation with a better standard of life. We see it play out even now, when a certain number of Instagram followers can mean you are offered freebies like meals at fancy restaurants or hotel stays. Gaining status in many ways can materially improve one's life, so why wouldn't we want that?

But, as with so many of the things we are conditioned to chase, achieving fame and status isn't an eternal blissful state either. Storr reminds us, 'There's no happy ending – we'll always continue wanting more because, subconsciously, one of the major things we seek is status, and status is always changing. You can't keep your status and lock it in a box. It can always decline – and other people can always overtake you.' It's only when we start to notice how much we crave status that we can wake up to how much the desire for it rules our lives. The question is: if we let go of our desperate need for status, will feelings of true success come more easily to us? Chasing status is in many ways a trap that keeps us from feeling truly successful in our own lives. Buddhist practitioner Jack Kornfield says that at the end of our lives, we are rarely asking, 'How much is in my bank account?' or 'What was my status like?' But more like, 'Did I love well?', 'Did I live fully?', 'Did I learn to let go?' Our desperation for status can often lead us on to the wrong path, the wrong partner or the wrong job. Our desire for status can encourage us to humblebrag our way towards external validation, but completely gloss over the fact that we are on the wrong track to true inner fulfilment.

When I was growing up in the noughties, with baby-boomer parents, celebrity was something people in my life seemed to look up to, or at least placed an importance on. Relatives would talk about celebrities like they knew them: 'What's Tom Cruise been up to now!' According to the *Atlantic*, 'Baby boomers made up the first consumer generation.

They grew up in the television age, watching mass media emerge from their living rooms, embracing sex-driven, racially integrated rock and roll – Elvis, Jimi Hendrix, the Beatles – all of it fuelled by the world's first true mass audiences.' It makes sense that people with consumerist parents might have also placed an importance on fame and celebrity growing up. From an early age I picked up on the fact that these celebrities seemed more important, as people listened to them, valued them and felt a connection to them. I saw the premium that was put on a famous person's opinion. Successful people: I wanted to be around them, amongst them, near them. It's no wonder I ended up working in the magazine industry. I was fascinated by celebrities and what their lives must be like. Every time I was in Sainsbury's with my mum, the other kids would saunter over to the chocolate and sweets, while I would run over to the magazine section and feast on the cover photos, wondering what these people's lives were really like behind the scenes.

Reality TV vs Actual Reality

Where baby boomers grew up in the television age, millennials grew up in the reality TV age. In 2000, the first series of *Big Brother* launched, and it soon became a household favourite and Channel 4's most successful programme. It was a new era of television that people at home just couldn't get enough of. According to the *Guardian*, the first season drew huge numbers of phone votes and online clicks: '20 million calls, with 7.4 million for the final, and 200 million page impressions on the website'. Then, in 2002, Will Young won *Pop Idol*. I was thirteen. At the height of its success, the show had 13.9 million viewers, more than 59 per cent of the TV-watching public. This is a dizzying amount of attention for one person plucked from obscurity. As an avid viewer, I didn't really think about the real people on the screen, just that they were living the dream! They were on the world's stage, on every front page, with audiences clapping and cheering wherever they went. This is what everyone surely wanted? They were the pinnacle of success and fame at the time. They were the chosen ones, with overnight status, notoriety, money and success. I used to have daydreams about winning a reality singing show. (I can't sing.)

Fast-forward to 2017, and I found myself at Will Young's home in London, interviewing him for my podcast. I remember him being barefoot, welcoming and friendly, as we chatted on his sunken comfy sofas, with dogs, books and art all around us. Of course, life is not always what it seems, even for the 'famous' amongst us. Since that day, Will has courageously opened up about his mental health, anxiety and past trauma, a poignant reminder that a taste of fame and 'success' does not make you immune to serious issues, and shouldn't make you feel silenced or unable to voice them.

I'm not sure what Will Young's definition of success was back in 2002, but when I asked in 2017, he said, 'I love pottering around my house. I love the fact that I've got the kind of job where I can do this podcast. I feel really lucky. It's Monday, and I'm still in my tracksuit. I don't work in an office. And I don't think I could. This is my life. I get to hang out in my house. Who made the rules?' Thirteen-year-old me, sat on the floor, watching a pop star win a competition, did not realize that the prize at the end of it would not be the name in lights, the arena tours, the swanky parties, but actually to be able to design your own day, hang out with your dogs, and learning bit by bit how to take better care of your mental health. A life pretty similar to mine, and maybe yours.

One of the most shocking celebrity stories to come out in recent years concerns another one of my childhood icons: Britney Spears. I idolized her, dressed like her and ultimately wanted to be her. She was the girl next door, the fun-loving friend. But if we fast-forward to 2007, there was a whole industry dedicated to mocking her mental health breakdown. 'If Britney Spears Can Make It Through 2007 Then You Can Make It Through This Day' was plastered across mugs,

T-shirts and keyrings. Some found this funny. But it was clear as day: the cult of celebrity was damaging our young talented stars more than we realized. Of course, we later found out that Britney had been kept against her will under a conservatorship by her father, which stopped her from making basic decisions about her life, including her own contraception and fertility choices. We had been witness to a real-life Margaret Atwood-style tale. Around the same time as Britney's public meltdown, gossip websites were constantly churning out horrific stories about celebrities – but it took a while for their intrusive 'journalism' to be seen for what it was: abuse. Even Perez Hilton admitted to being 'cruel' and 'purposefully hurtful'. In the noughties, being a 'celebrity' looked more and more like a hostage situation.

I have a tome on my desk called *Toxic Fame* by celebrity journalist Joey Berlin, written in 1996, which props up my laptop when I do Zooms. It contains thousands of quotes from famous people saying how awful it is to be in the public eye. In the introduction, he describes fame as 'toxic', 'a disease' and, interestingly, a 'self-imposed quarantine' that leads to 'loneliness, fear, self-doubt with corpulence, alcoholism and drug addiction'. There are some upsides and happy stories, of course, but the book is full of examples of why fame is not something to be idolized, including the fact cited on the first page of the introduction that 'the average life span of a celebrity is only 58 years, while the average for everyone else is well into their 70s'. It feels ironic to hear all these celebrities claim they don't want the popularity once they have it, often saying it destroys the joy of the work they went into the industry for. There is a sense, though, that no one really believes their claims. 'Why did you become famous, then?' is a popular retort, but I don't think any big celebrity quite imagined that they would become as famous as they are, or, at least, they didn't realize what exactly they'd be in for.

I've seen the negative effects of celebrity first-hand. I was recently at a book launch and a very famous, very noticeable A-list actress was there, with her trademark hairstyle and 'look'. The room fell silent when she walked in. She sat on the sofa eating snacks with her assistant and people awkwardly shuffled around her. No one wanted to say anything; they were too nervous. Nobody acted normal around her. When she went to leave, some of the bar staff followed her out, asking her for a selfie, and it was like she was an animal at the zoo, instead of just a person attending a book launch. It was the opposite of real connection. She didn't get to mingle at ease around the room, soaking up stories and shared moments. I felt grateful to be invisible on my Tube journey home. I put my headphones in and tuned the world out.

Not long ago, I watched a home tour of a famous model's

stunning house in LA – it was huge, and amazingly designed, with a personal bar, tropical gardens, a pool, multiple living rooms and beautiful balconies. Right before the cameraman leaves, the model says that recently she hasn't actually spent any time in the house at all, as she doesn't like staying there alone and she doesn't have any family or friends in the country. She looked really lonely, like a small child, as she stood by the door in her designer slippers. She might own this massive mansion thanks to her modelling career and celebrity status, but she didn't look happy, and she didn't have anyone to share it with. It was basically an echoey, empty home, albeit one with a good view. In that moment, the romanticism of living in an LA mansion, overlooking the Hollywood hills à la *Selling Sunset*, unravelled for me.

I feel lucky to have peeked behind the curtain of celebrity culture during my previous jobs working at magazines, and therefore to have seen beyond the smoke and mirrors. I remember going to the *Glamour* Awards in 2015, where Amy Schumer made an incredible acceptance speech, but I was confused at why none of the celebrities were really speaking to each other. I noticed a few random famous people pose for a photo in silence and then go back to the groups they were with. The next day, on the *Daily Mail* online, I saw everyone laughing and posing, and instead of thinking, *Wow, look at all these people who are friends having a great time*, as I usually would, I knew this time that the reality wasn't like that at all. It was part of their job. They were working, had posed for a few photos and then they went home to their real lives and families.

In the happiness chapter, I outlined a few things that actually contribute to our inner happiness, including solid warm relationships, strong connections and autonomy over your own life. In many ways the cult of celebrity denies famous people these things, as they are disconnected from the real world in a way that can bring on loneliness. They may doubt their friendships, asking, 'Is this person just in it for my fame? Do they want something from me? Will they compromise my privacy?' They are isolated and alienated in their gated houses, and have their freedom taken away as every small action has to be considered in order to protect their privacy and security.

Sometimes all the 'things' and 'stuff' around us can be one big distraction, papering over the cracks, stopping us from ever looking at ourselves in the mirror. There is a tongue-in-cheek line in writer Emma Forrest's new memoir *Busy Being Free*, where she is talking about the view from her old LA home with 'birds skimming the water' and 'little houses carved into surrounding hills'. She says: 'Why would you want to look inwards to fix things, when looking out brings instant relief?' This materialistic 'instant relief' can be a distraction. On the *Chase Jarvis Live* podcast, Martha Beck makes a point that feels culturally taboo in many ways, saying that some very privileged people can struggle to have an internal breakthrough because they have too many external distractions in the form of material wealth and stuff. They can attempt to 'cover up' how unhappy they are, because they have the means to do it. It's nicer to cry on a yacht than in a cramped bedroom, of course. Sociologist Max Weber talked about 'the iron cage': the more obsessed with status you are, the more trapped you may feel. Your life is better when you are not in survival mode trying to make ends meet. But people with all the 'stuff' will also go to great lengths to avoid looking at their problems, using behaviours and substances that allow escapism, from high-end shopping to continuing to upgrade their life. We all have a playground of distraction to prevent us looking our existential unhappiness in the eye; it's brave to look behind the curtain.

A New Type of Celebrity

During the pandemic, many of us saw celebrities in a different (perhaps slightly confusing) light. Yes, in the earlier months of the pandemic Gal Gadot and her celebrity friends sang a rendition of 'Imagine', a cringey attempt to try and 'help' a cause, while their Instagram Stories featured swimming pools in the background. Ellen DeGeneres sparked a backlash after joking that self-quarantine was like 'being in jail' (while she was sat in a mansion in Montecito). But, while we were in very different boats, we were all weathering the same storm. They were on Zoom (like us!), they let their hair grow out (like us!), and, despite their more luxurious surroundings, they didn't appear so untouchable. We were all in the pandemic together. On the whole, it did level the playing field in a weird way. Joe Wicks's workouts. Oprah doing livestreams. Sophie Ellis Bextor's kitchen discos. David Tennant and Michael Sheen's miniseries *Staged* performed over Zoom. They still needed jobs and we still needed entertaining. The magic had been broken and nowadays we're perhaps not so captivated by their star power. They are just like us (albeit with nicer things).

Nothing sums this up better than Kim Kardashian wearing Marilyn Monroe's famous 'Happy Birthday Mr President' gold dress to the Met Gala at New York's Metropolitan Museum of Art in 2022. Stars of the golden age of Hollywood, like Marilyn Monroe, were seen as being more than human: mysterious, untouchable and perfect as they glowed on screen. Kim Kardashian made her name through her reality TV show, where we are shown every little nook and cranny of her waking hours. The glamour has gone and is only now glimpsed at fancy dress parties. Even the Oscars doesn't seem to wow people as much, and with the viewing figures declining, it only serves to offer some light gossip to talk about with friends. I enjoyed the tweet by author Lindsey Kelk that said, 'Once again, I am forced to remind you that the Oscars takes place in a shopping centre.'

Sarah Manavis at the *New Statesman* suggested recently that we are in 'the age of boring celebrity'. Analyzing recent red carpets and celebrity behaviour, she said, 'Our era of celebrity demands safeness and sameness, a level of uniformity driven by social media, which rewards specific styles of images and being.' Social media might indeed have a part to play in this; the algorithms serve us the popular looks that then drive the trends people follow and buy. It seems like many celebrities are too afraid to be different these days. There hasn't been an iconic David-Bowie-as-Ziggy-Stardust or Lady Gaga meat dress moment for years.

Despite this waning interest in traditional celebrity, according to research from Pew Research, 78 per cent of Gen Z teens would be willing to share personally identifiable data in pursuit of online fame, compared with only 7 per cent of millennials. Gen Z have so many more role models now, who exhibit behaviours that help them make sense of their own values, rather than traditional stars who are only famous for their singing or acting, for example. Where millennials relied on traditional media like magazines and TV for their entertainment growing up, the younger generations are more online. According to recent figures, almost 50 per cent of teenagers use TikTok daily and going 'viral' is a common aim for users, who see it as a gateway to money and fame. Interestingly, a Think with Google analysis found that 70 per cent of teenage subscribers said they can relate more to YouTubers than to traditional celebrities.

The nature of celebrity has been changing since the evolution of the internet. We have direct access to the people we follow; paparazzi culture has less power, and celebrities are more outspoken about the abuse of power. Fame and recognition can be constructed via an iPhone, without the trappings of an industry to create it. We have more 'micro influencers' experiencing 'micro fame' now. The untouchable A-list celebrities who remain completely mysterious are dwindling in numbers (or being edged out of our collective attention by the constant onslaught of newer online celebrities) and those people don't need to represent or speak on behalf of everyone.

The meaning of fame is evolving, and while we know it means popularity, it also now means 'a platform' to make change. According to research centre Pew, while voting and traditional political engagement tends to be higher among older adults, '32% of Gen Zers and 28% of Millennials have taken at least one of four actions (donating money, contacting an elected official, volunteering or attending a rally) to help address climate change in the last year', compared with smaller percentages of Gen X and baby boomers. Gen Z have been shown to be more open and inclusive to different identity types (whether that's gender or body image), which may be driven by the increase in the number of famous activists they are exposed to online.

A 2019 study by Lego said that one-third of kids between the ages of eight and twelve aspire to be either a vlogger or a YouTuber. Even a friend of mine recently sighed over her glass of wine, 'I might just quit my job and start a bloody TikTok account if it's that easy and all the kids are doing it.' This is the general, slightly warped, consensus: anyone can start a TikTok or YouTube account in their bedroom, and anyone can become a millionaire. Obviously, that's not the case.

This new way of finding a large audience can inspire jealousy, with trolls wanting their slice of fame and fortune too. Or it can inspire positive change, with people like Zoella filming 'hauls' in her bedroom while also shining a light on issues such as bullying, sex education and screen time; or someone like the wonderful late Deborah James, a former teacher campaigning to raise awareness of bowel cancer, amassing over one million followers, raising over £7.5 million for charity and receiving a damehood for her activism. The idea of anyone being empowered to spread a positive message is the side of online 'fame' that many of us can really get behind.

We're in a democratic world of celebrity, which means more people can reach an audience than ever, rather than just a handful of celebrities that live in the Hollywood Hills giving us stuff to gossip about. Instead of big celebrity brands like Posh and Becks, we watch 'micro-influencers' with this same curiosity now: people with between one thousand and ten thousand very engaged and loyal followers. Statistics show that micro-influencers have a much higher engagement rate with their audience than traditional celebrities. We are more interested in those who appeal more personally to us and our interests: people who are more 'relatable' in the way they reflect reality. The influences on our lives aren't so limited nowadays and that can be a good thing (more choice and inspiration) and also a bad thing (it can be completely overwhelming).

Quoted in *Toxic Fame*, Ellen DeGeneres said, 'It really doesn't take much to be a celebrity now, so to me it's not much of a flattering thing.' I would claim this is even more true now; so many people can be famous in their own way that fame has almost lost its meaning. But it's also opened up the world of celebrity to a more authentic way of communicating. In one of her most popular videos, Emma Chamberlain, a Gen Z YouTuber with over eleven million active subscribers, talks us through a panic attack she's just had, which sounds very similar to my own experiences with them. She then tidies the kitchen, does some painting, has a bath, drives to her version of a health food shop, eats snacks while talking to camera and then lies in bed under a blanket with her cat. She looks a bit bored as she questions what to do with her day at home, but she gets excited as she talks about her evening plans: hosting bitesize interviews on the red carpet at the 2022 Met Gala. Her life is normal but also not normal. She interviews Riz Ahmed and they joke about crying in the toilets later. In her conversation with Finneas they discuss their impostor syndrome. She laughs with Amy Schumer about how they will google themselves during the ceremony. This is the new world of celebrity, more open and vulnerable, and they are gently mocking themselves. People are more actively engaged with influencers rather than old-school celebrities because they are letting us in and there is less mystery. They are more like us. (Even if they do live in mansions in the hills.)

But despite influencers being more open and vulnerable, it's important to remember that, like traditional celebrities, they're also at risk of putting on a mask and playing a role. In 2015, a young Australian influencer called Essena O'Neil made headlines for being one of the first influencers to come forward and say that her feed was one big, curated lie. We sort of knew it, but it was the first time someone had openly said it and written honest captions alongside the pictures. She would write the reality behind the photo (of her in a bikini on a beach, laughing) and re-edit the captions to reveal the 'manipulation, mundanity and insecurity' that was really going on behind the scenes. She also commented on her own behaviour and how she was playing into the same insecurities she would feel herself: 'I've also spent hours watching perfect girls online, wishing I was them. When I became "one of them", I still wasn't happy, content or at peace with myself.'

Like traditional celebrities, online 'celebrities' also often struggle to meet the pressures of being so visible. A 2018 piece in the *Guardian* looked into a stream of videos that were uploaded by popular YouTubers who were discussing their burnout, chronic fatigue and depression. Elle Mills, a twenty-year-old Filipino-Canadian YouTuber said, 'And why the fuck am I so unfucking unhappy? It doesn't make any sense. You know what I mean? Because, like, this is literally my fucking dream. And I'm fucking so un-fucking-happy.' The nature of the job meant she needed to post at the beck and call of her audience, and she explains that the constant pressure to upload and make content on demand was leading to anxiety and depression. This is the downside of working for yourself: if no one has taught you how to set boundaries, or if you are susceptible to poor mental health, it can be really difficult to say no, or take a break, especially if it is your livelihood. Traditional celebrities or bigger influencers have an agent – a whole team – around them to help them manage their workload and time, a type of system that has been in place for decades. Newer influencers who are still at the beginning of the journey may have to work out a lot of it themselves first, without the support of a team. It begs the question, who would want all of this? This isn't saying that these types of 'successful' online personalities have it worse than other people in society – far from it. It's saying that it's not the answer, either: that there is something wrong with our society that glamorizes certain lifestyle choices and makes us think they're a one-way ticket to everlasting fulfilment. We are forgetting what makes us happy on a very basic level, no matter who we are.

Despite the quietly abusive nature of an industry that tells people they are lucky to be part of it, I do understand why people might want to seek fame. Status brings validation, and it's natural that we're all seeking that. We want to be seen, understood and recognized. In some ways it can act as a safety net when it comes to getting work, especially if you work in industries that value status. *Times* columnist and author Caitlin Moran gave an insight into why people might crave fame that I think about often. Speaking in the journal.ie, she talked about three types of power you can gain within society, saying, 'There's infrastructure power, you're connected through the judiciary, the courts, governments, the NHS. The second is obviously capital, financial, businesses, people who inherit money and then reinvest it. And then the third power is fame, the reach that you have, the ways that you can change a life is fast and powerful.' These three ways to grow status are interesting: political power, financial power or fame. For people who might not have the connections or the financial privilege, fame can be a way of getting out of your situation or creating a new story for yourself.

But famous or not, we can all make a difference to a small group of people – we are all influencers in some way. We matter without an audience of adoring people. We don't need to chase outward markers of success or status in a big way to feel seen, as there are so many other ways to feel authentically appreciated and validated. The first step is seeing ourselves. Not through a lens, not through the eyes of thousands of followers, but really, truly seeing ourselves for who we are, and understanding what matters to us. Validating ourselves first is an important but overlooked part of building an authentic sense of status. When we crave the approval of others, really, we are craving our own approval. It is possible to achieve a new kind of recognition and do it well – and feel significant within a community without the lonely trappings of old-school fame. The key is building recognition on your own terms, having good boundaries and feeling appreciated by the people in your life, not strangers on the other side of a screen.

Chapter Reflections

1. **Take a look at your life from a distance.** Write down your life's story in ten bullet points. Not the details; the overarching themes. Celebrate how far you've come, and how much the story matters. Write about your life in the third person, as though you are a friend of yours; use your first name and not 'I'. What do you notice with some distance between you and the story of your life? What is going well? What are you proud of? What forward leaps (small or big) have you made?

2. **Who are you comparing yourself to, and why?** What kind of status are you chasing, and why? Use any feelings of jealousy as a useful emotion to see what you think you want, or what you feel is missing. It can be a useful exercise to figure out

what we feel is missing from our lives, and then
sit with it: ask yourself whether, in reality, this is
actually something that you might want, or if you
are comparing yourself to some else's status story.

3.   **What feeling would more status bring you?** It is
     human nature to want to chase status, but we can
     ask ourselves whether it is status we are chasing
     or validation? What is the feeling you desire? For
     example, would more status make you feel
     prouder of yourself? More loved or appreciated?
     How can your relationships and interactions with
     the people in your life help you to be accepted,
     safe and supported?

4.   **Celebrate a small achievement.** Maybe
     something that happened recently that you
     would have struggled to cope with a few years
     ago. Take the time to appreciate yourself (even if
     it's little and often) and see how this bolsters your
     sense of status. What are you most proud of
     overcoming recently? Keep a folder in your
     emails or a 'success diary' of moments that felt
     good. Celebrate yourself, before waiting for
     someone else to celebrate you.

SIX

The Money Myth

*'We buy things we don't need with money we don't have
to impress people we don't like.'*

DAVE RAMSAY

'Money doesn't buy happiness, because the best things in life
are free,' a multimillionaire boy band member said recently
in an interview I watched online. *No,* I thought, *don't give me
two cliches in one! If I had as much money as you do, then I would
be very content with my lot.* Then I looked at him closely on
the screen. He had bags under his eyes, and he was defensive, worried and insecure, telling the interviewer about
how the pressure often got to be too much. Huge amounts
of money came with the worldwide tours, but he said he
missed his home, his family and his old life. He looked
fidgety, while wearing very expensive designer trainers. I

didn't envy him. I'm sure many people would call for the tiny violins to be pulled out, but as we saw in the celebrity chapter, this story keeps being repeated. *Surprise: famous rich person turns out not to be very happy.*

I promise I'm not here to tell you that money doesn't matter. It matters, hugely. It's a fact that you can move through the world more easily with access to money. You can quite literally 'throw money at a problem'. Not all problems, but most. Life is much harder and more stressful without it. This makes money such an emotional topic. It makes most of us immediately clench up. Money worries can take up huge amounts of space in our minds. Money can make us scared, defensive, angry and stressed. In America, whether or not you get access to basic healthcare comes down to money. In the UK, how you are looked after later in life comes down to money. It can affect our living situation, health, childcare, sense of safety and the way in which we go about our daily lives. And, at the time of writing, we are going through a cost-of-living crisis, leaving households squeezed when it comes to even just the essentials, like food, clothes, fuel and energy.

Being financially stable impacts our wellbeing, full stop. If you don't have to worry about money, you are likely to be sleeping better, you are able to lead a healthier lifestyle, you are able to afford therapy; having money enables you to say no to things more, and you are able to improve your daily habits. Being financially stable is quite literally a lifesaver in some cases. As Chelsea Fagan, founder of *The Financial Diet*, said, 'Becoming financially stable will for most people do more to improve your mental health than literally anything else.'

But in this chapter, the key thing I want to get across is that becoming financially stable is a different proposition to our cultural obsession with becoming excessively wealthy. The subject of this book is success, and many associate being *very successful* with being *very wealthy*. From house tours to large Chanel handbags to helicopter rides to Rich Kids of Instagram, we see people's excessive lifestyles play out on social media and it's mainly digital voyeurism. If I were a young person looking at those lavish lifestyles, I might get confused and think that is the pinnacle of what success is. We are social animals, and we assume that flexing the things we have on social media will increase our chances of being accepted by the herd. As Jasmine Teer, vice president of strategy for Small Girls PR said: 'With social media, we can access a 24-hour rotating display of materialism and disparity.'

Interestingly, a 2018 study published by Sage Journals found that even though nearly 66 per cent of participants thought that signalling wealth or status would make them more attractive to potential friends, they found the opposite to be true. People who displayed high-status markers were found to be 'less attractive' as new friends than those with neutral status markers.

As said before, being financially stable will absolutely improve our happiness and wellbeing, but chasing endless amounts of money, always wanting more, feeling like we need to buy everything in sight, working in a high-salaried job at the expense of our mental health, isn't the big fix we think it is. It also doesn't make us connect better with others, as the study shows. There is a nuance to this conversation, and two things can be true at once:

- Money buys comfort and security: healthcare, food, a home, more freedom.
- Money doesn't buy happiness: you can have all of the above and still be unhappy, have struggles and be mentally or physically suffering.

Research backs up the idea that excess money beyond a point doesn't make us miraculously happier. A well-known 2010 study by researchers Daniel Kahneman and Angus Deaton found that people tend to feel happier the more money they make, *up until a point*. Once we hit around £50,000 (or $75,000) a year, the research shows we do not become happier the more we make. We should bear in mind that this research is ten years old; the equivalent amount would be higher now with inflation, and dependent on where you live and how large your family is. It is also worth remembering that this figure is much higher than the current average salary in the UK (according to the ONS, as of November 2022, the current average salary in the UK is £27,756).

The entrenched idea that happiness grows in line with ever-expanding wealth is a myth. Having a million pounds will not make you a million times happier. But having a certain amount more *would* increase our health and happiness. It is important to distinguish this, otherwise this elusive idea of ever-increasing success keeps dangling like a carrot on a stick, and we get sucked into a never-ending black hole that can't be filled.

On my podcast, sociologist Martha Beck said, 'Having one blanket and one fire makes us happy. One hundred fires and one hundred blankets does not make us one hundred times more happy.' Imagine it. With cars, for example. You are incredibly happy to buy a new car: you've saved up and it's shiny and new and you can drive to many different places. Now, imagine you have fifty cars lined up outside your home. Are you fifty times happier? Probably not. If anything, it would probably be overwhelming: expensive to maintain, too much to organize and a bit depressing because you'd have nothing left to aim for.

We must take a look at society's obsession with excess, and

the fact that many people in our modern world still don't have enough to feed themselves and their families or heat their homes comfortably. Magazines celebrate the 'rich lists' without really digging behind what that glorification of abundance costs us, global society and the environment. We glamorize money and wealth as the be-all and end-all to happiness. If the answer to all life's problems was money and a new thing, then we'd feel happy for ever after buying an expensive pair of shoes on payday. But it wears off very quickly. And then we forget about what we have and want another thing. And another thing. Therein lies the rub. It begs the question: what void are we trying to fill? What are we really chasing? What is behind our insatiable need for more? Why is excess painted as the meaning of success, and why do we rarely discuss what our personal definition of 'enough' feels like instead?

The 'Rich and Beautiful' Myth

I've been privileged enough to witness excess up close and personally. In 2007, a few months before my eighteenth birthday, a friend from school invited me on their family holiday. I said yes, and I quickly started to realize that this wasn't going to be your average holiday. This wasn't going to be camping in Cornwall, or a quick Ryanair flight to somewhere hot and sunny. Little did I know that this friend lived a very different life to mine behind the scenes; their family had a level of wealth I'd not witnessed before. This was a five-star resort abroad in the sunshine, somewhere they'd been going for years, with private chauffeurs from the airport, a cooling towel handed to me when I arrived at the villa, and a chef who would cook anything I wanted to eat from scratch. My seat was pulled out for me; even something as ordinary as a Diet Coke was handed to me on a gold tray. The shower in my en-suite bathroom had six different settings, and the bed had silk sheets. It was like being in an episode of *Succession*, before knowing this lifestyle even existed. Everything was luxurious, expensive, over the top, gourmet, the best of the best; it was like I'd been whisked away into another world. *So, this is how some people always live?* I thought. I couldn't believe that I was getting to see it all, like some sort of Secret Cinema immersive experience.

But a few days into the holiday, I came down with a vicious cold. My friend was furious with me because their parents had paid for expensive scuba diving lessons for us. And when we sat around the table having our five-course dinner cooked for us, the dad, a very successful businessman (who had retired aged forty-five after selling an early technology company), often spent the evening shouting. He constantly spoke loudly about his success. Over multiple glasses of wine, he would shout at his children to try harder, to work harder, and he was always pushing them to be successful like him. His wife went to bed early every night, probably to get away from the tension. I was in the most beautiful place I'd ever stayed, I was in visual paradise, and yet I couldn't wait to go home. The atmosphere felt thick and uncomfortable. No one was happy, and the more upset everyone became, the more money they spent to try and make things better. The more fights they had, the more oysters they ordered and the more wine they drank. More, more, more.

On that holiday, I stayed in bed, coughing and sneezing, reading *Affluenza* by Oliver James, which had just come out. The book's premise is that we are being riddled with a virus called 'affluenza', a portmanteau of affluence and influenza: 'An obsessive, envious, keeping-up-with-the-Joneses [epidemic] – that has resulted in huge increases in depression and anxiety among millions.' The words I read on the page reflected what I was experiencing in real time: people pumping money into their misery, spending their lives papering over the cracks and pretending it was fine, instead of whipping the carpet back and asking themselves, *Why is none of this working? Why do we keep thinking this pursuit of more will one day solve our problems? Why are we so obsessed with outward markers of success? Why do we think money will make us happy on the inside?*

I felt like I was learning an early(ish) lesson. *Do you want to be rich and successful, or do you want to be happy? What would it look like to be both? What exactly should I be striving for?* Society sells these outward markers of success to us constantly. A bigger house will solve your problems. A luxury holiday will cure depression. A new outfit will change your mood. Rich celebrities are the happiest people on the planet. I was in hell on that five-star holiday, staying with people who didn't listen to each other and were emotionally suffering. I felt lonely and constantly on edge. I disliked it: I disliked the company, I disliked the posh hand soap and plump designer cushions. I felt ungrateful, and then I felt guilty. I was supposed to be enjoying this. *This is what everyone wants, isn't it? Isn't this the social media dream?*

On the flip side, remembering my camping holidays as a young kid, with mud slushing under my flip-flops, terrible toilet facilities and tents that blew around in the wind, my heart swells. We had so much fun: we sat around campfires, we went swimming in the sea, we flew kites, we went on walks, we went rock-pooling, and every moment was filled with love for each other. We had more fancy holidays too, but, crucially, I felt loved, supported and happy regardless of the setting, regardless of the thread count.

Taking on board Maslow's hierarchy of needs, more money means more comfort. Once we have air, water, food, shelter, employment and a sense of connection, everything else adds on bonus after bonus. Money brings ease. Accessible health-care. Up-to-date gadgets to help run a home. On-demand childcare. Luxurious food. A first-class flight, speedy board-ing. A leather-seated taxi with ice cold water, a five-star hotel room. Once we've had a taste of these things, we may find it hard to go back. We get used to it. Your self-perception is changed and therefore money still rules your life, only in a dif-ferent way than it does if you are just trying to get by. Striving to maintain a life of luxury is a trap that no one really speaks about. It is a myth that there is any magic money formula that makes all of life's problems vanish in an instant. The myth is that excessive amounts of anything will keep making us happier and more in control. But no one, regardless of what they have, is actually in total control. It's an illusion.

A friend of mine who works in property, finding homes for the uber-rich, says she doesn't see very happy people: 'It's a weird thing to say, but they look really unhappy and trapped. Most of them have no time to spend in their homes, yet they buy or rent these totally extravagant properties as a status symbol. They never spend any time in them. They are constantly stressed on the phone, worrying about their finances.' When I watch *Cribs* or *Selling Sunset*, it feels like the extravagance wears thin for people quite quickly. Once you have enough money to live in a warm home, pay your bills, support your family and buy some nice things, beyond this, it's just a lot of extra fancy wrapping. No one *needs* to live in a sixteen-room mansion. No one *needs* to be a billionaire. These are not the paths to happiness we think they are. It's important to talk about, because we currently live in a world where a homeless citizen crisis still hasn't been solved, where people still don't have enough to feed their children or heat their homes. A practical solution to this that is being discussed around the globe is universal basic income: a government programme in which every citizen would receive a set amount of money regularly. If everyone were to have a foundational amount of money, enough to get by, then everyone would have their basic needs met, which is a good starting point to thrive from. Cynics believe it might make people unmotivated, but optimists (like me) believe it would encourage people more than ever, because they wouldn't be bogged down with other major struggles in their lives. Imagine if we stopped striving to make our lives look so perfect on the outside, papering over the cracks with material things, but started looking at ways we can change the system, so we *all* have access to enough. Food banks should not have to exist in our modern developed society. We could focus on making ourselves feel better on the inside. Imagine a world where wealth is not just measured by what's in our bank accounts from our jobs, but in time and energy for all of us. This form of wealth doesn't cost the earth (literally) and reaps far greater rewards for everyone.

Money and Success Don't Always Mix

We often conflate status, success and money, when they aren't as closely linked as you might think. I've noticed a phenomenon which I'm going to call 'career catfishing' (a term I might have just made up), where the reality of a situation doesn't match up with what is being touted. There are plenty of people who become very visible and therefore 'successful' in the eyes of society, but who don't have the finances to match. This confuses us, because we expect such people to have money. We grew up seeing rich pop stars and film stars on our screens, so we equate visibility with financial success. But as the nature of celebrity has changed, there's much more diversity in who we see on TV and on social media. For example: an activist on the news who doesn't earn anything for their campaigning; authors still waiting for royalty cheques months after publication; an entrepreneur struggling for their next round of funding; or an influencer with a million followers who has no advertising revenue.

At a writing retreat a few years ago, I met a YouTuber who was extremely famous and successful at what she does. We were a group of around fifteen writers or 'creators' who had been invited to learn more about how to write and sell a script, and at the time she had around five million subscribers. We had all met beforehand to get the Tube to the venue together, and she was looking around a lot, clearly nervous about being spotted by one of her fans, which was a common occurrence. In our eyes, she had 'made it' – she was a success story.

When we got chatting for a long time, late into the night, she was really open about the fact that she made hardly anything financially from YouTube itself. She had very little money and was struggling to pay her rent at the time. It surprised us all. Then, later that week, I read a piece about an American internet star who made so little money from her online pursuits that she had to get a job in a fast-food restaurant, from which she was subsequently fired because her boss said it was distracting having so many fans coming into the restaurant. The irony of being dragged down and left unemployed by your own success. Today, there are more outlets for monetization than ever, including OnlyFans, Substack and Patreon, but it's still not exactly easy to get paid for all the work you do, no matter how successful you might look from the outside.

A recent coaching client said she was out of sorts because she perceived herself to be a failure. She was a successful chef, but she wasn't yet making any money from it, and was earning a living in other ways (writing, consulting, work-shops). When we dug into it, she realized that she did actually feel successful by her own standards. But through the eyes of strangers or 'society' as a whole, she didn't think she'd made the cut because she wasn't making money just from being 'A Chef'. She'd let a panel of made-up people that lingered in the back of her mind affect her sense of worth. She underestimated the value of feeling successful on her own terms and of allowing herself room to grow. She realized that she *was* making money from her passion, just in a slightly different way than she had imagined. Sure, she wasn't running her own restaurant yet, or a TV chef, but she was doing it, and she was making it work. Being paid to do your hobby or passion all day is certainly one version of success, but focusing solely on this can make many of us feel compelled to constantly compare ourselves to others. There are many other ways to feel rich: in time and fulfilment. We *do* need to earn money, but we don't have to just earn money from our passions for them to matter. We must understand that the money we make – or don't make – (and where we get it from) is not an indicator of our personal value, and it's up to us to celebrate lots of different forms of success.

Our relationship with money, interestingly, is also about our *perception* of how much money we have, compared to other people. If you had a certain amount of money and you got by fairly well, and you had no way to compare your life to anyone else's, you'd probably be pretty content. The minute we go on Instagram or hear about a colleague's promotion or see a neighbour with a better house, car, everything – that's the moment when we begin to feel we simply don't have enough and want more, which is completely natural. According to the Institute of Labor Economics, 'Over time the long-term growth rates of happiness and income are not significantly related. The principal reason for the contradiction is social comparison. At a point in time those with higher income are happier because they are comparing their income to that of others who are less fortunate, and conversely for those with lower income. Over time, however, as incomes rise throughout the population, the incomes of one's comparison group rise along with one's own income and vitiates the otherwise positive effect of own-income growth on happiness.' Fascinating.

Excessive amounts of anything will never fill an internal human void, and, in fact, the impact of excess wealth has an enduring negative effect on people. Much like what we explored in the Celebrity Myth chapter, *Psychology Today* reported that the offspring of very affluent parents have 'disturbingly high rates of substance use, depression, anxiety and eating disorders'. There is a clear problem here which isn't being discussed because it's so embedded in our society that money equals happiness.

Our Endless Pursuit of 'More'

At the time of writing, all over the world there are wildfires breaking out, glaciers are melting at a faster rate, droughts are becoming longer and tropical storms more severe: a stark reminder of climate change. And there's one main culprit: greed. As the *Times of India* states clearly: 'Unsustainable consumption is the fundamental cause of pollution and ecological destruction.' It's a clear fact: we consume too much.

The author Sherri Mitchell uses indigenous stories and their deeper meaning (which have been often ignored, or stereotyped, by the Western world), to shed light on the cost of our consumer culture. She explains how we are all interconnected, and that whatever you spend your money on directly impacts people for better or worse. When we acquire something new, we rarely think about the people working in the background for that item to arrive easily into our hands. We don't think much about the individual workers who grew the food, packaged the food or delivered the food. We might feel like we need convenience to run our modern lives smoothly, but the increasing speed of creation and consumption harms both the planet and the people working to sustain our lifestyles. For example, it might look outwardly 'successful' to have all the new fashion trends hanging in your wardrobe, but the billion-dollar fashion industry still pays garment workers poorly. If we want to spend our pay cheques on stuffing our wardrobes with the latest fashions, it might be wise to remember that Pretty Little Thing's parent company, boohoo, has come under scrutiny for allegedly paying its factory workers as little as £3.50 an hour.

In her book *Sacred Instructions: Indigenous Wisdom for Living Spirit-Based Change*, Sherri tells the folklore story of the dance of the cannibal giant. She explains it as 'a figure within our mythology who lives deep in the forest and sleeps throughout time, and only awakens to one specific cry of the earth mother. That particular cry lets the cannibal giant know that human beings are harming the earth mother faster than she can heal and they are consuming faster than she can produce. So the cannibal giant dances the people into this hypnotic state where they continue to endlessly consume at faster and faster and faster rates until they consume themselves off the earth.'

Do we really want 'more, more, more' when it literally costs us the earth?

Time and Money

Whenever I think of the word 'currency', I immediately think of that exciting feeling of galloping up to a bureau de change desk to convert your pounds into euros before going on holiday. But there are so many other forms of currency and value exchange, and so many other forms of 'wealth' we should learn to balance in our lives. In the dictionary, currency is defined as 'a medium of exchange for goods and services'. Money of course is society's main method of exchange – but there are so many other currencies that we fail to consider, even though they are each important in their own way.

Your time is also a currency. Your energy is a currency. Your mental wellbeing is a currency. So is your happiness, concentration, generosity, influence, enthusiasm, skill set and so on. We go through life exchanging one thing for another every single day without even thinking. Tit for tat. You scratch my back; I scratch yours. You do the dishes; I'll do the laundry. If you pay me, I'll do that job. Research says we are reciprocal by nature. If someone does something nice for you, you'll probably be compelled to do something nice back. Mostly everything is an exchange, and it doesn't always need to involve money.

Traditional self-help books constantly offer advice on growing, scaling and smashing it. They send the message that we should be trying to get to the top as quickly as possible. There is nothing inherently wrong with wanting to make shedloads of money, but we need to interrogate the reasons behind that desire. For some people, earning slightly less can actually free up space to live a more fulfilling lifestyle.

As Melanie Eusebe, author of *Financial Wellness*, told me, 'People may be making a lot of money, but they've locked themselves into a lifestyle where they're not happy because it's not necessarily what they want to do with their time, so that's why I always relate time and money together.' Money is important, but so is our time. The most precious resource there is.

Of course, the maths matters. Making £100,000 and working forty hours a week, for example, is not the same as making £100,000 and working eighty hours a week. When you're looking at jobs you also need to suss out the company culture so that it also lines up with your preferred lifestyle. How much money do you make per hour when you break it down? Is there something you wish to change about your current ratio? Is there anything within your power that you can do?

Sometimes, we forget the choices we do have. Perhaps we

don't check in with ourselves often enough or give ourselves credit that we have the power to make even very small changes to our lives.

I spoke with Joshua Roberts, author of *Generation Drift*, who changed up his career following a nervous breakdown in an outrageously stressful job. He told me how it felt to have made that decision and then accept it: 'I don't have children and I'm not a full-time carer, so I do have a degree of freedom that other people don't have, but everyone has more freedom than they think they do. When I worked for big companies, I used to make more money than I do now, and I do struggle with my friends having posh houses, but I also don't want to kill myself any more. So, given that rather bleak trade-off, I'm happy with the deal that I've done.' For lots of people, the cost to our mental health of working too hard is literally not worth it, and it is no longer an option to continue pushing ourselves beyond our means. When digging deeper into this topic of money, Joshua found that having lots of money did not automatically equal better health: 'Some of the most fascinating research I did was with the bankers at Goldman Sachs or the partners at KPMG who were earning a million quid-plus a year but were miserable; they couldn't sleep and had problems with eating. How many times do we need to be told that having lots of money doesn't make you happy before we'll believe it?'

Emotional Debt

We have to make sure we are filling ourselves up enough at the emotional well. Burnout occurs essentially when we go into emotional debt. Here are some examples of unequal exchanges:

1. My job looks great on LinkedIn, but it's depleting my mental health.

2. The money is good, but the job will take me away from my family for weeks at a time.

3. The promotion is good for my career progression, but it'll take me away from my passion projects.

4. My friend lent me money, but he may use it to exert power over me.

5. The restaurant gave me a free meal and now wants endless social media mentions.

It doesn't need to be 100 per cent 'fair' to be the 'right' exchange – friendship exchanges, for example, are rarely completely equal – it just needs to be something you're happy with, that feels worth it to you. I had a good job in a nice office. But the exchange (the average salary at the time) wasn't worthwhile because the hours made me ill and I completely lost interest in the work itself. I left to go freelance and, yes, the first year was tough. I had to find my feet and earned half of my previous salary. I had to make sacrifices and cut back on so many things I'd got used to. But the exchange? Freedom to control my calendar, less stressful mornings, space to breathe – the exchange felt fair and right. I felt rich in time and space for the first time ever. The exchange was no longer overly skew-whiff. When we are out of balance everything goes pear-shaped, and it is a sign to review things. Less money at first didn't bother me, even though I had to make material sacrifices; I was no longer sacrificing my wellbeing. I was also in my twenties, so I was able to cut back on things a little more easily. Now, I make sure I am aware of the things I feel I 'need' vs what I actually do need. It helps me make informed choices over the work I take on. I no longer take on projects with overly demanding clients who expect constant overtime, who are rude or impact my wellbeing with their ways of working. Some exchanges are no longer worth it to me, and I would rather take on different jobs that pay less, or jobs that enable more flexibility. Of course, we can't always hand-pick the work we do, but even being aware of my energy exchanges and boundaries has made a huge difference to my life.

The small decisions we make each day are important. At the end of the day, they all constitute how we spend our waking lives. We trade different forms of currency at different moments. We might get 'paid' in different ways: in time, connection, freedom, space. Understanding this can help us break free from the money myth and allow our perspective to broaden, revealing different goals and ways to find meaning. As psychologist Emma Hepburn says, 'Being time-wealthy (having time to do what's important to you) is much more likely to increase your happiness than being wealthy.'

A good way of thinking about it is that money *itself* doesn't actually mean that much to us. It's the things we can do *with* the money that hold a deeper meaning. Most of the time, now living in a digital world, we don't even *see* our money. We exchange it for things through a tap of a card, or a transfer across wires. Hepburn also says, 'Using our money to connect to what's important to us, or having time to do what's important, has a far more powerful impact than having more money or stuff.' It's what we do with the money that matters.

We might have an attachment to the numbers in our bank accounts, pounds racking up in an investment account, a faraway pension, or money tied up in stocks and shares, but only because they give us a feeling of safety. I had a huge feeling of happiness when I bought my house, because I knew living with my husband there would bring me joy and safety. I felt secure. It was a psychological transaction as much as a financial one. Money is the pathway to tangible circumstances *and* a feeling state.

Spiritual teacher Byron Katie's clients are not living on the breadline, but many of them feel miserable and desperately still want more money. She encourages a meditation exercise to stop us thinking (or worrying) about the past or thinking (or worrying) about the future, and instead gets us to think about right now, in this very moment. You sit quietly for ten minutes. She asks if everything is OK now? Do you have enough in this moment? Do you have 'enough' to get through the next hour? The next day? Once you ask these questions, many people might insist that they do indeed need 'more' from a practical point of view, perhaps to pay for their dinner that night, or, in a broader sense, for their life in general. But many more people realize this: they have everything they need right now. This isn't about not wanting a better life for yourself (we should all strive for a better life in our own way) but being aware that, past a certain threshold, your happiness or contentment will not increase further just based on the extra things you acquire. We have a chance to be happy now, which can lead to being happy 'then' too. Our obsession with *excess* is the problem here, as it creates a cycle of feeling we never have enough. It creates a lifetime of chasing, of never having enough, of never ever being happy. This is about creating your own sense of 'enough'. It's about starting somewhere. It's about taking back control over our lives in the here and now, as well as having the space to dream and scheme for a better life too. It's about being aware of the things that are constantly marketed to us, and knowing deep down that we can have our own goals that matter more than society's excessive definitions.

Chapter Reflections

1. **How much money is enough *for you*?** How much would you need to be able to do the things that bring you the basic happiness and freedom in your life? What things do you love doing? (Refer back to the things you wrote down in Chapter Two.) It can be empowering to simply be aware of what you need in your life, and what you want vs what you think you want, and splitting them out.

2. **Why is money important *to you*? What does it allow you to do?** What does money represent, and what do you want it for? There is no right or wrong when it comes to money and what we personally want (whether that be a nature reserve

or a yacht), but it helps to make sense of the 'why', so that we don't get lost in more, more, more without a clear reason in mind.

3.   **Do you ever feel financially trapped?** Outside of the obvious outgoings, are there any things that make you feel uncomfortable (e.g. a friend who always books expensive restaurants without asking you, or a hen-do you just can't afford to go on)? Work out your own money boundaries, and what would make you feel better. Have a brainstorm privately with a partner or close friend, or with a coach, around ways you can unshackle yourself from what you think you 'should' say yes to, and the things you actually want to prioritize.

4.   **Outside of money, what are the things that make you feel successful?** Money is a great indicator that things are going well (and, as we've discussed, very important too), but write down a list of things that are going well which don't have a monetary value. In what other ways do you feel 'rich' in your life? What things light you up that cost you nothing?

SEVEN

The Ambition Myth

*'It's getting increasingly harder to tumble out of bed
and stumble to the kitchen and pour myself a
cup of ambition.'*

@KATMCGOLDRICK

I recently bought a print from artist Mr Bingo's website, an image of a set of steps going up and up and up, before a precipitous drop at the end leading to the word 'death'. I had it framed and hung it in my office as a reminder that death is the only certain conclusion to all our striving and 'climbing'. Sorry if that might sound bleak, but I find it strangely uplifting, and a reminder to enjoy each day instead of constantly looking ahead. You can climb all the ladders you want, but ultimately we all end up in the same place. Someone recently reminded me that most funerals only last between 30 and

45 minutes, so whenever you are worried about whether you're achieving enough, just remember that the highlights of your life will be summed up in less than an hour. Quite the eye-opener, and a reminder that *most* things are not worth worrying about. You are in a moment of your life now, and soon you will be in another moment, and you won't think too much about the small blips. If anything, it reminds me to keep going, keep trying, remain present, ultimately not to take anything too seriously and to make sure, no matter what I'm doing, to try and enjoy myself along the way. You're doing so much better than you think you are.

In terms of climbing steps or ladders, many of us have been on the general ascent, not entirely sure where it's all leading to. School, university, exams, internships, jobs, careers, successful careers, and then – what? I've noticed there's a collective shrug when you reach a certain point and think, *Hang on, wait a minute – where does all this climbing and striving actually lead?* What if there isn't anything up there? Why are we spending our time so stressed in the pursuit of more success when we have zero time to smell the roses? In this chapter, I want to turn this existential crisis into something positive. If the idea of success equalling happiness is a myth, then how do we decide how to spend our lives? What would happen if we collectively pushed back on the societal expectation to keep climbing and climbing for the sake of it?

Do we ever actually sit down and ask ourselves: *How ambitious do I really want to be? What is 'enough' for* me? As journalist Lisa Miller acknowledged in her 2017 piece about millennial career women called *The Ambition Collision:* 'After a lifetime of saying "yes" to their professional hunger – these are the opportunity-seizers, the list-makers, the ascendant females, weaned on Lean In – they've lost it, like a child losing grasp of a helium balloon.' I do feel like I'm finally letting go of my helium balloon. I'm letting things drift away naturally, rather than clutching at them desperately. Perhaps the raw hunger for success fizzles out eventually, like a candle that burns brightly and then slowly flickers.

When we talk about shifting ambition, we can't ignore the impact of the Covid pandemic. Of course our outlook has changed since going through a collective traumatic event like that. We've seen that anything can happen, and that life is short, so a reassessment is only natural. We have stared down the barrel of our lives and thought: *What am I doing? Do I even like my life?* Our relationship with ambition has changed, more subtly for some, and quite drastically for others. In her popular essay 'Where Did My Ambition Go?' Maris Kreisman asked, 'Where does ambition go when jobs disappear and the things you've been striving for barely even exist any more? And what if the things for which you've been striving no longer feel important?'

Post-pandemic, the *New York Times* published an article called 'The Age of Anti-Ambition', with the tag line 'When 25 million people leave their jobs, it's about more than just burnout.' During the pandemic we couldn't avoid the fact that jobs were labelled 'essential' or 'non-essential'. As we saw in the productivity myth chapter, many people realized their jobs were meaningless, with anthropologist David Graeber's term 'bullshit jobs' entering public discourse. We were literally told in black and white that the world could survive without us tip-tapping our keyboards or putting jokes into Slack. Being ambitious no longer meant a shiny LinkedIn update, and a successful life was suddenly starting to look very different. People started thinking, *Maybe my life's ambition isn't about sitting in an artificially lit cubicle farm. Maybe there is another way.*

In 2022, I worked on a campaign with Google which revealed that a staggering number of people (50 per cent of all UK adults) were re-evaluating their friendships, romantic relationships and work lives more than ever post-pandemic. Searches for new courses, such as printmaking or film directing, were up, and huge amounts of people thought about pivoting their careers into something more fulfilling. A 2021 *New York Times* article, 'Welcome to the YOLO Economy', talked about a cohort of 'exhausted, type-A millennial workers' who spent years 'hunched over their MacBooks, enduring back-to-back Zooms in between sourdough loaves and Peloton rides', and are now 'flipping the carefully arranged chessboards of their lives and deciding to risk it all'. This sums it up well: a group of people who were told, 'If you work hard, you'll reach your dreams!', when really the dream they were sold turned out to be just living in front of a screen, churning out work for other people. We bought into the career dream but, instead, the conversation was turning in on itself. Maybe reaching your 'dreams' looked more like working less, or working differently, and a YOLO generation of workers were born. Workers who found creative ways to earn money, thinking less about the outward-facing appearance, more about the cash they could make in any way possible while travelling with a Wi-Fi connection. The 'dream' started looking different for us all and we realized that the cookie-cutter definition of 'career ambition' wasn't all that glamorous or shiny.

Ambition, Back Then

What did 'ambition' used to mean to me? Let's rewind. Growing up in Exeter, in the pit of my stomach I knew from a really young age that I wanted – needed – to burst out of the confines of my home town. It was a lovely place, with everything anyone would ever need, and was even voted 'best city to live in' in 2018. It is a happy, secure, well-run small city, where for many the dream of nipping to the shops in your nice car, before parking it outside your house with a garden and enough space to breathe, feels well within your grasp. It has good cinemas, a big library, a lively arts scene, plenty of parks, atmospheric music venues, nice enough shops, restaurants, a cathedral green, and beautiful places to hang with friends, like the eighteenth-century inn with outdoor seating on the banks of the canal locks. Who wouldn't want to live there?

In many ways, it was the perfect place to live, and I feel very lucky to have grown up there, just less than half an hour's drive to some of Devon's most beautiful beaches too. But something pulled at me, telling me I had to leave, the minute I was old enough, the minute I could. I guess my own brand of 'ambition' meant doing the Dick Whittington thing of packing up my belongings and going it alone in a new, bigger city. Bigger dreams, bigger places, bigger goals – whatever that meant to my young brain.

I look back and wonder why I wanted this so desperately from an early age. Why did I lie on my bed googling 'Soho Square', scrolling through photos of high-rise buildings late at night, even though everything looked harsher, the underground was dingy and crowded and people in the photos looked stressed? When it comes to our own relationship with ambition, I often wonder if the grass appears endlessly greener. In many ways, now I am slightly envious of the people that stayed in my home town, or at least those who enjoy a slightly quieter life in whatever form that takes. There is something about living in a big city like London that turns even the most basic of errands (like finding a dry cleaner) into an episode of *The Crystal Maze*. The set-up of smaller towns or villages can feel simpler and more stripped-back in a way that supports community. There is an incredible energy to a city of people chasing 'the hustle', but it doesn't exactly feel calming.

My ambitions to leave my hometown weren't better than other people's, just different, but looking back I'm glad I did it on my own terms. Ambition is a personal thing, and only we know what we want, or at least what to try. I've heard so many stories from people I've met on my book tours who tell me they didn't feel they had agency over their ambition growing up. Ambition was forced upon them, they felt, by their parents, by society. You *will* get good grades. You *will* go to university. You *will* get on a graduate scheme. You *will* keep climbing. Baby-boomer parents are known for instilling a strong work ethic and wanting the best for their kids. My parents never pressured me (beyond just wanting me to do well for my own sake), and I was surrounded by people who

told me anything was possible. This guidance and empower-
ment around pursuing what you want to is a benefit of a
great education or great parenting. Not 'you should', but
'you CAN'. Pushing yourself to be more ambitious can also
come from being scared about your future and the state of
the working world. At university, I remember a tutor inter-
rupting a lecture to remind us that there was a recession,
none of us were safe, and that statistically only 20 per cent of
us would probably get a job. This of course fed into a sense
of scarcity, but also ambition.

Into my twenties, when I was still figuring out my relationship with ambition, the media and culture around me
impacted me hugely. I would soak up the feminist rhetoric
of the time: a popular slogan told women that AMBITION
ISN'T A DIRTY WORD! It was blazoned on T-shirts and
tote bags, along with 'The Future is Female' and 'Girls Just
Want To Have Fun(damental Rights)'. The eighties to the
noughties was the age of 'career porn'. Sexy, shiny jobs filled
our screens: *Working Girl* (1988), *Sex and the City* (1998–2004),
Legally Blonde (2001), *The Devil Wears Prada* (2006), *Mad Men*
(2007) – the list keeps on growing. *On the Basis of Sex* (2018)
recounts Ruth Bader Ginsburg's journey to becoming former Associate Justice of the Supreme Court of the United
States, which made me want to bring down my enemies,
wear all-black and take over the entire world. My heart was

racing coming out of the cinema after watching that film. Experiencing feelings of big ambitions can feel so overwhelming and incredibly exciting.

Sophia Amoruso's book *#GIRLBOSS* first came out in 2014. It documents how she founded the fashion retailer Nasty Gal back in 2006 from a MySpace store, how she bootstrapped it to $30 million in annual revenue and eventually scaled the business to over $100 million. She was on the cover of *Forbes* and listed as one of America's richest self-made women next to Beyoncé and Taylor Swift. She played the game for a bit, milking her success, delivering workshops, doing talks about 'how to be successful'. In the end Nasty Gal folded and was sold to boohoo. I loved the word 'girlboss' in my twenties. I loved Sophia's story. I loved her energy and determination and how she built a business by herself, starting with just an idea and a MySpace account. I came close to putting 'girlboss' in my bio. I was fully sold. I remember discovering the pastel pink book in a store on a trip in New York and demolishing the whole thing in one sitting, on a park bench. I wanted to be a girlboss! For me it wasn't so much about the word but a mood, a feeling, a sense of *Fuck this, I can do things my own way.* An identity. A movement. I was like a moth to a flame. But even though the girlboss message was empowering, the shiny exterior of the woman in the pastel suit never really showed the whole picture. Even though it was encouraging women to start businesses, pitch their ideas and get funding – in a time where fewer than 2 per cent of female founders secure venture capital – it was just a label. The behind-the-scenes effort of growing and scaling a business was hardcore, but it had turned into a simple, shiny badge of honour to be your own CEO. The idea of the girlboss was too superficial, too dream-like. We saw many women with their arms crossed in power-woman pose on the cover of *Forbes*, but it glossed over the real work and the realities of what it took to become 'successful'.

I remember bumping into an acquaintance (I'll call her Sally) and she looked knackered. She had launched an app, and on Instagram she looked like the epitome of a girlboss. But in real life, she was exhausted and suffering from health issues. The app was going well, but she was spending all her time pitching; she had no time to actually do anything enjoyable. She also had to work much harder to get funding than her male counterparts. The idea of the girlboss captured the millennial woman's heart, but the hashtag didn't quite equip us with the tools for a long-lasting, nuanced version of success. The problem with being a girlboss was that it was too narrow, too confined, too 'trendy'. It didn't incorporate the true breadth and diversity of women's capabilities and the many different versions of success. It was like a cardboard cut-out. The conversations around the girlboss did not take into account other intersections such as race or class. As Rosamund Irwin said in a piece in *ELLE*, speaking of the girlboss dream, '. . . the reality often fell short of that dream – particularly in terms of inclusivity. Only a select few ever seemed to win, and they came from the same mould: photogenic, social-media savvy, stylish and – usually – white.' Being a girlboss was like trying to be Barbie: it wasn't intersectional, it left people out, it was too perfected so no one could ever truly win. We can't win when we are not able to be ourselves. Even Sophia Amoruso has had enough. She tweeted, 'Please stop using the word Girlboss thank you', in June 2022. Even she is redefining what success means all these years later, like we all are.

All through my twenties, I watched these #Girlboss-type women sitting on panels for International Women's Day, and it felt like the worst thing you could say was that you weren't ambitious. It was trendy, inspirational and cool to say you wanted to take over the world, empower yourself and others, and reach for the moon. Build a unicorn. Raise millions. Employ hundreds of people. Open offices in every capital city. It would make you a bad, guilty feminist, if you admitted to having little to no ambition or, God forbid, wanting a big lie down. We were meant to be going after the big opportunities! There was all this talk of the 'glass ceiling' and pulling up a seat at the table and asking for more. Many women before us busted a gut to get access to all this so it made sense to go in all guns blazing. It felt like a taboo to not roll up your sleeves and start 'leaning in'. So even women who were not inherently ambitious were forced to behave ambitiously. Women I knew who wanted to stay at home with their kids felt shame. As I've outlined in this book, all definitions of success are valid, and all definitions are worthy of celebration. It's time for us to refuse to be narrowly locked into what success and ambition are 'supposed' to mean.

So, what does ambition look like to me now? These days, when I go back to Devon, I take in the seaside views, the walking route sights, and realize I'm back where I started, the same person as I always was, underneath the 'ambition' scratching at me like a hungry puppy. I can breathe out now, the restlessness seems to have gone, or at least softened and slowed. Ambition is no longer something I want to feast on unnecessarily. According to a study by Bupa Health, our drive and ambition peaks at the age of thirty-three. At the time of writing, I'm three months away from turning thirty-three. When I told a coach friend of mine I was moving away from traditional metrics of success, she said, rather cryptically, 'Ah, you're going into phase two.' Phase two: an important part of the journey. (More on that later.)

So, the revelation that I am no longer actually that ambitious has been strange to come to terms with. I'm ambitious up to a point, clearly, but right now, I don't feel it as intensely at all. It's gone. Shrivelled up a bit. It might not look that way to the outside world, but I can't locate it as easily. There was a shift and it didn't feel like something I was necessarily in control of. At first it was difficult to admit, as though it was shameful. What happens when you don't actually want the things you're 'supposed' to want? How do you grapple with wanting less? How do you quell the anxieties inside you that you might be letting people down? Or letting yourself down? How do you come to terms with the fact that you're turning down opportunities that people would kill for? Admitting your own lack of ambition can be scary, until you unpick where those feelings even come from in the first place.

Our Ambition Is Not a Fixed State

My friend Daisy described the aftermath of the 'slay it' era as 'tottering through the wasteland of the girlboss apocalypse', which made me laugh. I imagined us walking around a barren land, holding broken high heels, asking, 'What the hell was all that about?' Even though we had girlboss books and phrases like 'the future is female' on our T-shirts, we just still aren't there in terms of the equality we keep talking about. The wage gap has remained steady for a decade, and according to Crunchbase, global venture-capital funding for female founders dropped from 2.9 per cent to 2.3 per cent in 2020. It's even less for Black women, who receive less than 0.35 per cent of all VC funding. Women all over the country are still being penalized for telling their bosses they are pregnant. It happened to Joeli Brearley, founder of campaigning group Pregnant Then Screwed, who explains in her eponymous book that '54,000 women a year are forced out of their job because they dared to procreate, and three quarters of working mothers face workplace discrimination. And this was before the pandemic, with its never-ending cycle of extraordinary childcare challenges and overt pregnancy and maternity discrimination, resulting in a tsumani of mothers exiting the labour force.'

As we saw in Chapter One, due to the way our qualities are perceived, women tend to be over-represented in certain types of caring or public-serving roles, whereas men are more likely to have an element of autonomy in their remit, even if they are in a low-paying job or are self-employed (for example they still made up 99.19 per cent of the technicians, mechanics and electricians in the workforce in 2021). Work seen as traditionally masculine (high status, loud, visible) is rewarded, while women tend to be the 'helpers' in their households or to support their spouse's business without having a sense of ownership. Lisa Miller sums it up in her Ambition Collision piece: 'It's as if the women have cleared spaces in their lives for meteoric careers, and then those careers have been less gratifying, or harder won, or more shrunken than they'd imagined [. . .] Women enter workplaces filled with ambition and optimism and then, by 30 or so, become wise to the ways in which they are stuck.'

I've always been trying to operate outside the rigid systems that uphold this inequality, and to define ambition for myself by running my own business without the need for funding. When I wrote *The Multi-Hyphen Method*, published in 2017, I wanted to work in a different way, and move away from an identity that was tied up in one job. I wanted the freedom to have multiple interests, and to not have to commit myself to one job title. My message got conflated by some reviewers with hustle culture, ambition, growth and money. As though the ambition narrative has shifted from 'corner office goals' to a pressure to be entrepreneurial 24/7. Some people thought I was demanding that everyone must have a side hustle on top of their stressful job. This wasn't my message at all.

Not everyone wants their own company, or to juggle multiple businesses. Not everyone has to monetize their side projects or grow their 'brand'. Some people love these opportunities provided by the internet (me included), but we forgot to make the small print readable: it's OK not to want the same thing as your friends, peers or strangers. It's OK if your definition of ambition looks different. Yes, I wrote about multiple income streams and balancing multiple interests, but really it was about redefining ambition for yourself, in whatever way works for you. Being a multi-hyphenate means you can design your own career and work week. Work a four-day week if you like. It means you can experiment. It means you can swap projects in and out. It's a way to establish what success looks like for us, rather than everyone else, to work on different projects, try new things and piece ourselves together like a quilt. Multiple income streams could look like making enough money to live a digital-nomadic life, or it could mean a Warren Buffet-style strategy. This was my way of carving out my own definition of success, while other people may want a 9-to-5 and a clear-cut distinction between work and life (even though I believe it is important for everyone to have boundaries, regardless of work set-up). The goal is to figure out what you want, and that might be something completely different to what your friend or an online personality wants. We can be ambitious in the ways we fight for the life we want to have. Ambition doesn't have to mean one thing. Our ambition changes as our lives change, and so does our definition of success. It may not stay exactly the same over the course of our lives, and that is OK.

It's also OK to be a barrel of contradictions when it comes to our sense of ambition. Most people I've chatted to about careers in daily life and on the podcast – from bosses to publishing execs to magazine editors to celebrities – flit between 'world-domination goals' and wanting to live a quiet life in a cottage by the sea. We spend a lot of our lives going between these two parallel worlds, wanting more, then wanting less, then not knowing: mothers who love their kids but want freedom; people who travel the world but miss their bed; people who want to be in a relationship but not to have to compromise. It's normal to want nothing and everything all at once, or totally different things on different days. To go in and out of things. It's not all about upwards growth. I've realized I'm ambitious about living a good life. Not ambitious for ambition's sake.

Company of One

Paul Jarvis's book *Company of One* is a refreshing take on how bigger is not always better. It examines the ways you can have a happy, exciting and even entrepreneurial life by avoiding growth. When Paul left the corporate world, he realized the world of high-profile work, scaling strategies and always wanting to be the best was just not his personal idea of success. Now he works in his own way and lives a more rewarding life. I am no longer interested in this dogged pursuit of making my goals bigger and achieving more just because it is what I 'should' want. I want to stay where I am. I want to maintain what I have; my goal is not to grow and scale and take over the world. I could hire more people, strategize harder and invest more, but I look at others in my industry who are doing 'better', selling more books, earning more money and having fancier experiences, and a part of me shrugs: that's cool for them. I want to slow down and look at what is already working. I want to enjoy what I'm doing in the moment, rather than make everything a goal to be smashed. I no longer want to be a girlboss on a mission for world domination.

Just Run

I have been getting into running lately, and it's interesting how I went about it: I didn't say that I wanted to 'go for a run', I wanted to be *a runner*. I wanted to buy all the posh gym kit, download the Strava app, tell my friends about my runs and be able to run alongside the other runners. I felt like I wasn't very active, and I liked the idea of having something else to strive for, outside of work. So, I went for a light jog one Saturday afternoon, spotting dogs running away from their owners and doing whatever they please, noting how the leaves were changing colour on the trees, breezing past people on dates walking awkwardly side by side. Then, I got a stitch and simultaneously ran straight into a horde of racers in hi-vis activewear taking part in some sort of weekend race, checking their pacing on their Apple Watches. All very well for them, but I suddenly felt really self-conscious. Who was I, trying to run on the weekends? I looked down at my Strava app, which told me I'd only run 2k, a measly 2k. I felt run-down and lacked energy. I trudged home dejected, where I picked up Sarah Moss's novel *Summerwater* and came across this passage: 'All that chatter about minutes and seconds and splits and Personal Bests, are we not measured and recorded and found wanting often enough already these days? Why not just run?' I breathed a sigh of relief, my shoulders dropped, I put the book down and said it to myself: *Why not just run?* I realized that I had done *something* and, for that day, reminded myself that it was enough.

Farrah Storr, who is forty-three, and the former editor in chief of *ELLE*, wrote a piece called 'The Importance of Being Mediocre' in which she talks about her love of gardening: 'Gardening was mine and mine alone. There was no performance with this hobby. No end goal. No metric of success other than, I suppose, do I enjoy it? And even enjoyment isn't quite the right word, for enjoyment has its own never-ending metrics. I suppose gardening brings me a modest sort of happiness. It focuses me. It releases me from my head and my nerves. And that is quite enough.' Allowing ourselves to be mediocre in our hobbies might also help us chill out a bit when it comes to our careers.

When I interviewed author, musician and podcast host Cathy Heller about ambition and career, she made the point that we often forget there is a wide spectrum of success. Most of us fall into the middle ground, and there's nothing wrong with realigning our ambition to match that. In a world that is obsessed with fame and 'superstars', she believes in taking your ambition and making it work for you. Working in the music industry, which is very competitive, she realized she didn't need to reach the top to make really good money and have her music reach a large audience: 'I think for a lot of people, they believe that it's all or nothing. So, we fool ourselves, right? We underestimate ourselves; we overestimate what's actually there. And we don't know where we fall in all of that. For instance, it's like, oh, yeah, I have a liking towards music, but it's either Beyoncé or nothing. So . . . I will work in the insurance world.' Why do we sabotage ourselves by feeling so much pressure to be 'the best', when being good enough is absolutely enough? Many people totally give up on their dream because they already know they won't be the 'best'. What's wrong with doing it anyway, especially if it gives you joy? I recently enjoyed a BBC clip with Trevor Nelson interviewing singer/artist Ms Dynamite. She said, 'Someone asked me, would you prefer mainstream success or underground credibility? I'd say underground credibility all day long.' Success really doesn't have to be worldwide adoration. It can mean doing the thing you love doing in your own way.

Just before the pandemic, in 2019, I had already started noticing that so many women I admired – of all ages – were not as interested in the endless 'glamour' of their high-profile jobs. We've seen how Farrah Storr loves her gardening, and she told me how she now enjoys living in the countryside with her dogs and working remotely. Jo Elvin (fifty-one) former editor in chief of *GLAMOUR* is now a CEO of a charity, having left the magazine industry, and Lorraine Candy (fifty-three), former editor of *STYLE*, often shares photos of herself wild swimming in Cornwall. None of this is very *The Devil Wears Prada*, and there's no sign of a sterile, white corner office. I often wonder if Hollywood is to blame for our romanticization of these jobs, just like Disney made us romanticize princes with their white horses.

I remember someone once giving me this advice: 'If you don't want your boss's job, you should probably get out.'

Meaning: if you don't want to climb up the rungs of the ladder you're on, then you should get off it. But this is another myth. I am starting to realize that there is nothing inherently wrong with staying where you are. Maybe it's OK not to want your boss's job. Maybe it's OK to sometimes plod along and enjoy the smaller moments of life without needing a big plan. I quite like the advice that if you don't know what to do, sometimes the best thing to do is nothing. No drastic decision has to be made.

We are always changing, and what we want in life changes more than we think. This is the problem with being too busy to notice what your inner compass is telling you. I've lost track of the number of people who tell me that they just kept their head down at work and when they looked up five years later, they suddenly realized their whole value system had changed and their career just did not make sense any more. Most of us hardly ever tune into what our bodies are telling us; we push through it for the sake of ambition and we end up ignoring what we really need.

The Successful Feeling of Saying No

You'd expect anyone to be over the moon to get a promotion. The moment when all our hard work and striving is finally recognized, and we move up the ladder. But I have always had an issue with the idea and analogy of the career 'ladder', because it suggests that a career has to go upwards, whereas when I look back, the best decisions of my career have been sideways moves. Viewing it instead as a career 'jungle gym' has been totally transformative, and those moves have often boosted my joy levels, based on moving down or sideways or wherever my gut was telling me to move. As I described in the Money Myth chapter, when I left my agency job back in my twenties, I took a pay cut and a demotion, and I moved *down* the ladder. This was one of the most definitive points of my entire career. I moved from the agency world into the writing world, and yes, I earned less money, and there were a few sacrifices, but I could still pay my bills. I didn't go out for dinners with friends, I cancelled my Netflix account and various other subscriptions, I didn't buy any new clothes, my online grocery orders became much more savvy, but I was finally on the path I wanted to be on. What was the point in having all that extra money if I was miserable? I'm not saying that it wasn't difficult to begin with, and I had to find ways to earn more money alongside the magazine job, but if I'd only viewed success through an 'upwards' lens, I would have missed out on this opportunity that ultimately led me to a better place – not to mention the chance to write this book. As a quotation from the classic philosophical Chinese text *Tao Te Ching* by Lao Tzu says, 'Success is as dangerous as failure. Hope is as hollow as fear. What does it mean that success is as dangerous as failure? Whether you go up the ladder or down it, your position is shaky. When you stand with your feet on the ground, you will always keep your balance.' When you are moving towards your own definition of success, you will feel more balanced than you ever have before.

At a certain level, a promotion might mean you are moving further away from the reason you took the job in the first place (which can mean lower levels of satisfaction and motivation). With a promotion comes more responsibility, and not everyone enjoys managing others. So, we can find ourselves earning more and climbing the ladder, but not feeling fulfilled because of it. I spoke to Kim, thirty-three, a secondary-school teacher who realized that a promotion took her away from the classroom the majority of the time. 'Very quickly I realized that I really missed working with the pupils, and all the laughter and enjoyment of being in the classroom with them. I also missed teaching my subject and felt that a more administrative role didn't suit me or give me the same sense of job satisfaction that I had in my un-promoted role as "just" a classroom teacher.' She wanted to go back to being with young people, when her days were filled with more laughter. I loved her point about how not everyone needs to be the same: 'Every industry needs people who are ambitious and hungry for promotion, and to climb up through the ranks – but it also needs people who are content when balanced on the lower rungs and want to excel at what they do there.' Kim had been able to identify what success actually meant for her personally: 'Success is having a job you enjoy and actually want to do (at least the majority of the time); making a difference to other people; having supportive and valuable friendships; and experiencing contentment with your life, not always striving for something more.'

I spoke to Sanoobar, a marketing manager in a not-for-profit organization, who was offered a big promotion as an incentive to stay in her company after working there for years. She admitted it was the 'logical next step', but there was a 'but': 'When I was offered the promotion, I didn't jump for joy, and in my gut something just wasn't right. I began to question why I was staying there and if I was truly happy.' She said the thought 'terrified' her. When she asked her family and friends for advice, they were very honest with her and said in the last couple of years she had become visibly work obsessed and had literally disappeared. 'I was working twelve- to fourteen-hour days, checking emails on weekends, waiting for that notification "ding" like my life depended on it, and staying in touch whilst I was on leave. I hit a low point when I was on a beach in Dubai and FaceTiming my manager to reassure him that I had a plan in place already for an event that was happening. I was on my honeymoon, and I had made that level of keeping in touch OK.' She knew deep down that taking this promotion would mean even more misery and stress, and she was already physically and mentally exhausted. 'I couldn't take on more people to line-manage, and, despite their reassurances, more money just didn't seem worth it.'

I asked her about her definition of success now, three years on from turning down the promotion, and she said she feels like a different person. 'The thought of commuting to faraway places and constantly having to show my face just sounds exhausting. Money and success are not drivers for me any more. Success for me growing up was to have a very senior management role, make lots of money and live in this huge house and retire by the time I was forty. Success now is peace of mind. I want to work somewhere where I feel valued, in a role that I am happy in and where I feel like I am giving back. I want a job where I can log off at five p.m. and spend time with my family without the guilt of checking my emails under the duvet at ten p.m. (yes, I have done that!). Success for me is being content in my life, having a bit of extra income to use on the fun things in life and have the space to experience life when I am on holiday. This pandemic has taught me the value of time with my friends and family, and no amount of money will make me give that up now. I want to be present in conversations, instead of checking my work phone under the restaurant table. Traditional success feels like a lot of pressure now, more than it used to be.'

Quit to Succeed

Then there's stepping away altogether. In July 2021, young Olympian Simone Biles was making headlines across the news and trending on Twitter for 'withdrawing' from the Tokyo Olympics. It felt like a watershed moment, not just for Simone but for everyone watching, because we were experiencing someone putting themselves first, over and above a goal. Over and above striving for success. Culturally, and in the media, we don't see this very often. Instead of gunning for gold without any self-awareness, she said to the world, 'I have to focus on my mental health and not jeopardize my health and well-being.' Personally, I felt like this powerful admission was a permission slip for all of us to do the same. The subtext to me sounded like: *You know you have a choice, right? You know you don't have to push yourself to the limit at the cost of your health?*

Quitting is having a moment. In 2022, Holly Whitaker, bestselling author of *Quit Like a Woman,* launched the *Quitted* podcast alongside friend Emily McDowell. Each episode centres around stepping away from something, ranging from social media to alcohol, from being the boss to self-optimization. The podcast reframes quitting as saying no to something that is causing you to suffer and saying yes to yourself instead. Quitting because you're running away from something you're afraid of but want to do means you're hiding, but quitting when you know something's not right is empowering and worthy of celebration.

Quitting has been seen as a sign of weakness for so long: admitting that we couldn't handle something. 'Don't give up' was definitely drilled into me at a young age. But quitting is slowly being rebranded: quitting something that no longer serves you is a sign of strength and something worth acknowledging. I've realized a lot of my ambition, my 'drive' and my determination stemmed from fear. Fear of ending up unemployed (graduating into a recession), fear of being a bad feminist and fear of not really amounting to anything. Fear of not being enough. My ambition was also coated in insecurity too – chasing achievements used to be a way for me to feel seen by others. I used to think an achievement or accolade could make me feel more loveable, to others and to myself. Ambition turns slightly darker when we use it to beat ourselves over the head. We tend to use it as 'conditional love' towards ourselves. Whereas quitting can actually be a sign that you are taking your life back into your own hands.

'Upper limiting', coined by author Gay Hendricks, is when you hit a limit on your own happiness or success, and your fear or ego bring you back down to your own comfort zone. You may think you don't deserve a certain amount of success, so you will sabotage yourself so that you're back within the lines of what you feel comfortable with. I have realized there is a difference between 'upper limiting', whereby we hold ourselves back out of fear, and happily accepting that we do actually have a limit. Now, when I try to explain my own sense of 'enough', people around me don't always believe me. 'No! You do want more! You want to reach for the stars, you're just scared!' But the truth is niggling away underneath: I don't actually want all the stuff that people are expecting me to want. People get confused when you don't want the things you're 'supposed' to. Like not wanting children, or not wanting to be on TV, or not wanting to live in a mansion. Those aren't my personal goals. What's wrong with not wanting to keep achieving more and more? What's wrong with saying, 'I've reached a place I'm happy with, and I'll put my things down here for a while'? In fact, it's super-empowering.

True success is about perfecting the tension between being content with your lot, and also wanting to continue to improve your life. I like the idea of these two things coexisting. Being anti-ambitious in the traditional sense doesn't have to mean doing nothing – it can actually mean putting a pause on the endless hustle for nebulous goals and having a narrower focus on creating a life with intention. Ambitious in a new way. I spoke to writer Anna Myers, who recently wrote an article about why she believes contentment is better than ambition. She had big ambitions in the world of celebrity and used to work for Taylor Swift's publicist. Despite apparently having a 'dream job', surrounded by all the glamour and the success, she lost herself to the hustle. Then something clicked, and she realized what might be waiting on the other side. Contentment is a feeling we might associate with being older: something that comes once we're retired, like we have to earn our stripes before we dare say we're content. So, I asked Anna, twenty-eight, 'How do we practically strike this balance between feeling calm and content and aiming for those bigger goals?' Anna says, 'I try to set big, expansive, heart-led goals and make sure they're the kind of things that actually light me up, not just *what everyone else says I should want* or *what looks really good on paper*. I write them down; I know exactly what they are and why they matter to me. Big goals; little chasing, you know?' It reminds me of one of my favourite lines: high hopes; low expectations. We can have big dreams, but we don't have to burn ourselves out to get there; life is (hopefully) longer than we think, and we don't always need to be in a rush.

Nowadays, I'm having more nuanced conversations with my friends about ambition and noticing how many of them lean closer to quietly admit that they don't actually want to be a powerful CEO, and that they don't want to wear a power suit and hustle until they drop. They want to work a bit, have a good enough job, take care of themselves, and some would prefer to be at home with the kids more. Many are also realizing that it comes and goes. Sometimes it's time to rest more, and sometimes they feel as though they have a rocket underneath them and they want to go for it.

I am curious as to why many people feel like they have to whisper their dreams and ask permission, just because their dreams look slightly different to the traditional version of 'having it all' (whatever that means). One friend recently quit her impressive corporate job, and as her partner is a top earner, she is able to do more in her local community and raise her kids without working in middle management again. Another friend wants to work four days a week. Another wants to work less and is OK earning less. Another friend wants to earn six figures and work remotely doing so. Someone else I know quit their job as a top publishing executive and another wants to leave London to work in a bookshop by the sea, on less money. Another friend sold everything and is sofa-surfing again aged fifty. These choices come with sacrifices of course. In many ways, they also come with having the privilege and means to step back a bit. But ambition looks different to all of us, and I hope that finally we are starting to discuss this more openly.

Recognizing the limits of your ambition is a breakthrough moment. It's a release that allows you to have fun and just try things out instead. Fun, experimentation and curiosity are three of the tools I most value in my work now. These tools help me to grow, to spread the message I want to spread, just not in the way capitalism wants me to grow. They help me connect rather than conquer. One of my favourite sayings is, 'I'm not here to win, I'm here to contribute.' I first heard Seth Godin say this when I was in my twenties, and I thought, *Yeah yeah, Seth*. We all say, 'It's the taking part that counts' to kids so that they don't feel wounded. But more recently I have found myself feeling proud of my contribution. No one gets out of here alive, so why are we so obsessed with the 'winning' part? I'm happy to contribute, make space for others and show up. There is no part of me that wants to strive for being the very best. It sounds stressful. It sounds hard to reach for, and then even harder to maintain. This form of collective ambition feels stronger and warmer, and it suits me a lot better. I no longer need to win the race.

Godin also talks a lot about doing work for others, being in service, showing up and making a difference. His definition of success is no longer getting to the top of the *New York Times* bestseller list, but doing work of value, for a smaller number of people, showing up and 'turning the lights on' for others to fulfil what matters to them personally. 'Ambition' meant something specific growing up – it meant striving, climbing, scaling, growing. Now there is a different kind of ambition in the air. One that still involves growth, but not to the detriment of our wellbeing. It is a collective, or service-led form of ambition. In business terms, collective ambition is often described as all employees sharing the same sense of purpose. It's success as a team effort, like the way the whole of the England women's Euro 2022 team won the tournament, not the individuals who scored the goals. The former New Zealand prime minister Jacinda Ardern said it well: 'Economic growth accompanied by worsening social outcomes is not success. It is failure.' Ambition and success shouldn't be for the people already at the top – ambition should be about making everyone in the communities around us more successful too.

Ambitious Boundaries

Finding the right balance of ambition means understanding our boundaries. If we want to maintain our ambition while being content with what we've got, we need to rebrand 'growth' as a way to enjoy our lives instead of wearing ourselves into the ground. Sarri Gilman's 2015 TEDx talk on boundaries spells this truth out brilliantly, as she explains that success and ambition are often equated with saying yes to everything. Sarri used to run an agency that helped teens who were homeless, and she explains that she was 'deeply committed to it'. As the company grew, it demanded more from her. 'So what if I was on calls seven days a week, twenty-four hours a day, year after year after year? So what if I was getting sick [. . .] and had post-traumatic stress from it? Until one day, I was sat in this dark movie theatre, and I was crying and crying. I broke. And as I listened to my tears, I understood I couldn't keep running this organization that I started and I loved, my compass was saying no for my wellbeing. My wellbeing? Up against all these kids who need help?' Her guilt was not allowing her to acknowledge the seriousness of her burnout. But then she had a lightbulb moment, realizing she could still help without putting her health at risk: 'Then I understood: it had been my purpose to *start* the organization, but ten years later, the community could take care of this organization.' She sat with her board of directors, moved the new leaders over and onboarded the new team. And it's still going, over twenty-five years later. She encourages us all to tap into our 'yes' and 'no' compass. If we override our compass, we will burn out. This story is a great example of rebranding growth as a way of enjoying our lives, not just ticking off our endless achievements on paper. The world doesn't have to fall on any one individual's shoulders, and it's about using the collective ambition of a group to carry an important message forward.

A lot of us are starting to become ambitious in different ways. Ambitious for a better life. Ambitious for a healthier life. Ambitious on our own terms. Many people's ambition is changing from being ego-led (me, me, me, and my achievements) to being service-led (am I being ambitious for others, my family, a cause, a wider reason, something bigger than myself?).

It's only natural that we start off being ambitious in whatever form that takes. I was motivated by revenge when I was young, wanting to prove mean teachers wrong. Perhaps there is an element in needing to feel starry-eyed and spurred on by whatever it takes when we're young. We have energy, we have dreams, we have big plans, and we also want to chase status. It's also then normal for our ambition to wax and wane at different life stages. As we get older, our ambition morphs and often it can shapeshift into a more collective version, a bigger goal than just the individualistic idea of success. Collectively, it feels like we are pushing back on the definition of ambition (i.e. endless productivity) that society has dumped on to us and making room for what ambition really means to us. This is the important bit: our ambitions are personal, and often it takes some soul-searching to realize what they even are. And no matter the size of your ambition, there is no right or wrong answer.

Chapter Reflections

1. **How has your relationship with ambition changed over the years?** Has your idea of ambition changed since the pandemic? Write down what you wanted before and after 2020, notice what has shifted, and acknowledge how it will continue to fluctuate over the course of your life.

2. **Growing up, what did ambition mean to you?** Who or what influenced your ideas about ambition (were there books, films or people)? We can start making sense of our own definition of

ambition once we know where our thoughts originated from.

3. **What do your ambitions look like now?** If you didn't care what anyone else thought, what would you want to achieve?

4. **Do you have a more private definition of success?** Sometimes our truest wants and needs are things we don't feel comfortable sharing just yet while we work them out. Write it down, even if it seems very unachievable or nonsensical. Maybe one day you'll look back and it'll become clearer to you.

5. **What do you feel ambitious about, outside of work?** Are there any goals, big or small, that you feel excited about outside of traditional career ambition that you're not quite ready to tell anyone about yet?

6. **What 'micro-ambitions' do you have?** Forget long-term goals or any grand plans. Write down any small things you'd love to achieve, over the next day, week, month. What are the smallest steps you could take to achieve them?

EIGHT

The Tickbox Myth

'Societal norms and traditions are just peer pressure from dead people.'

SARA TASKER

Have you ever fantasized about having your dream job by a certain age? Or dreamed of a big wedding, followed by the perfect two children and a white picket fence by the time you were thirty? Does everything match up to how you imagined it would as a young child? If so, you are in the minority. Things rarely go as planned, and even if they do, sometimes our wants and needs change without much warning. We all have a list in our heads of the things we 'should' be achieving with our life. It is human nature to believe we will experience the things on the traditional tick list of life – marriage, kids, job – but we rarely stop to think about what we actually want.

We've seen how our ideas about happiness, ambition, money and work have been informed by the culture we grew up in. But what about the specific life moments we chase along the way? We think that by achieving a significant milestone we will be successful, and therefore happy. I want to show that these, too, are embedded social ideas, and we need to remind ourselves that we don't *have* to participate if we don't want to. In this chapter I'm going to deconstruct some of the most popular 'life goals', and help you think about what's right for you. It's time to stop going after the things we are 'supposed' to want, and to aim for things we actually do want.

The philosopher René Girard hit the nail on the head when he said, 'We want what other people want.' We are social animals, and it's in our DNA to want to rank and rate ourselves against other people. I like to think I'm becoming less competitive, but even as I walk down my street, I'm looking at my neighbours' houses and noting what plants, tiling and even what kind of front door they have. We look at what other people have and size ourselves up against it; it's part of who we are. Martha Beck recently explained it in a nutshell on Maria Shriver's podcast *Meaningful Conversations*: 'The reason we're so obsessed with social media and positioning and everything: a lot of that is our biology. We are really just a few shades north of baboons, in terms of our evolutionary development, and baboons are obsessed with hierarchy and will drive themselves to exhaustion to get higher in the troop.' It's no surprise that we often find ourselves comparing our lives to those of others, chasing an endless list of things that we hope will one day pay off. We assume that ticking off one more thing will mean we've 'made it'. It goes back to the 'status game' again.

But this is only setting us up to fail. We are risking disappointment if we expect our lives to slot into anything that resembles something neat and tidy to the outside world. Most of the time, life isn't wrapped up in a neat bow; it is messy and changeable, because we are always growing. In the July 2021 issue of UK *ELLE*, author Abigail Bergstrom wrote a piece asking the reader: 'Are You an Inbetweener?' She writes about those 'messy in the middle' bits, which she calls 'liminal spaces'. These liminal spaces are a natural, normal part of life; they are those times in between the solid life milestones. You might be living in a house-share that very much doesn't feel like 'your' house yet, or pregnant for the first time (a mother-in-waiting), or be between relationships, or be between jobs, or be between big life decisions. Although this is what most of life is made up of – especially when you're younger – these times can feel really difficult, because our human nature wants us to cling on to the things that feel definite: *Who am I? What's my job? Where do I live? How can I label myself?* It's understandable why we chase the feeling of being 'settled', and other people can find our 'in-between-ness' awkward too. At a family gathering, when some random relative asks you how life is, they want a neat, clean answer because it makes the social interaction easier for them. But even when you get to a feeling of being settled, those moments are often fleeting, because there's always something unexpected that throws us off course, or something nagging at us, making us want to shake things up.

I also want to question why feeling 'settled' is the goal anyway? We are conditioned by society to believe that bedding down into a routined safety net of a life is 'success', whereas most of life is messy and unplanned. Carving out a 'perfect' life that stays put and never shifts is just not realistic. In her piece, Abigail writes, 'People can view this limbo state as negative because we're in a culture that wants us to constantly progress.' The irony is, that by going through the limbo, we *are* progressing. The main message here: give yourself a break. You're doing great, even when it's hard.

Myth: Our Friends and Family Always Know What's Best for Us

We want to believe that the people closest to us know what's best for us. We go to them looking for validation, which can feel a lot like love sometimes, so we're easily swayed by their opinions. But a lot of the time they can be wide of the mark. Whenever I do workshops or talks, the thing people come up and say to me most often is: 'The thing is, I would do this, or give it a go, or change my job, but my parents/friends/family wouldn't be pleased.' Many people don't want to disappoint their parents. Many people admit they only went to university because it was the 'done thing' in their family, or because they felt like they couldn't pass up the opportunity if they were the first in their family to go. Many of us place a lot of importance on impressing others, impressing our loved ones and making the people around us proud. As nice as this sounds, it can also be quite damaging, as we are living our life on somebody else's terms. We are putting other people's needs above our own. Then the cycle often continues.

Seth Godin is very inspiring in terms of living life by his own standards. If we could bottle his inner confidence and sell it, we'd be on to something. When I asked him who he takes advice from, he explained that he has a small group of people who he could take feedback from, but in general, 'I listen to almost no one. And I learned that the hard way, because I used to listen to everyone. And most of us still have scars from high school. Because in high school, everyone has a voice, everyone gets an opinion. And so, we change how we dress and we change how we walk. And we change how we talk, hoping to please everyone, to fit in all the way. And that is when we stop trusting ourselves.' This is the key part: learning to trust ourselves, which is a long-term journey, not an overnight fix. He realized that sometimes the people who love us the most will put us off going after our dreams, often by accident: 'So what I discovered is that people who care about you will generally try to dissuade you from shipping creative work ["shipping" is a word Seth uses which means sending your work out into the world]. Because they don't want you to be hurt. And so, the industrial regime persists, because parents or in-laws or friends or whatever want you to get "a good job" with "a good company" by going to the [careers] office [. . .] But that doesn't mean that they're actually supporting you on the journey you truly want to be on.' By 'wanting what's best for us' other people often get it a bit wrong. You don't have to listen to your family, as well-meaning as they may be. Listening to our inner selves is the key, and the practical points at the end of this chapter will help you go about doing that.

Myth: Success on Social Media Is Everything

Nowadays we don't just seek validation from our friends and family in person, we seek it online, which complicates the matter even further. In my twenties, I was very good at presenting an image of success online. Author Lodro Rinzla calls it 'success theatre'. In that girlboss way, my social media channels were dedicated to showing off my achievements, like a glass cabinet in a high school corridor filled with trophies. Despite my performance of success, and how I made it look as though I was constantly on cloud nine, I knew the truth of it. It reminds me of the company Fake A Vacation: you send them photos of yourself and your family and they Photoshop them into exciting, desirable locations. For an affordable price, you could be standing in front of the Taj Mahal in no time – and without the long, dehydrating flight. Bargain! It's easy to fake anything these days, especially online.

It's hard to pull yourself away from the performance when everyone's doing it. People joke that a successful life moment hasn't even happened unless it's been shared with the masses. A friend who does not have followers and doesn't work in any public capacity recently asked me about what her social media strategy should be regarding announcing her pregnancy. It feels almost burdensome to have to project your success as well as just live it out. But it's a vicious cycle: the more posts about major life moments we see online, the more we want to emulate other people's achievements. Many of us feel a strange compulsion to art-direct the highlight reels of our lives and share them with others, otherwise, did they really happen?

Who knows the reality behind the journey to get to that 'success' post on Instagram? Has it been an overnight success, has it been hard-won or has it been a load of smoke and mirrors? As Jamie Varon says in her book *Radically Content*: '. . . what is impressive and glitzy can be fabricated. Followers can be bought on social media. Press placements are now overwhelmingly paid for. A "perfect" life might be overridden with debt. The perfect house looks so good on an Instagram post but on month nineteen of overstretching to afford it, does it feel good?' It's hard to step back and think, *What's really going on here?* when scrolling through social media, but it's important to note that things might not be what they seem. The well-known, much-quoted phrase 'Everyone is fighting a battle we know nothing about' seems to be more relevant day by day.

Influencer culture rubs success in people's faces and it can be hard to stomach if we, too, are trying our best and not enjoying the fruits of our labour or getting as many freebies. As I've said before, I do think the internet has levelled the playing field in some ways, giving us opportunities we might not otherwise have, but it can also make us feel robbed – *Why does my peer get that, and I don't?* As we know, there are many different factors which make up success, but comparison seems to be harder to stomach when you're looking at someone who seems to have all the same qualities as you.

Thirty-two-year-old former lawyer Olivia realized just how much social media was playing a part in 'filtering success' and making it all seem so easy, be it having a baby, buying a house, or achieving a promotion. She told me that social media had really made her feel alienated, as she felt she wasn't living up to these endless displays of outward success: 'It can feel isolating in a WhatsApp group full of baby chat, and during the pandemic when friendship catch-ups were conducted on Zoom, the focus was on engagements, a friend's bifold doors on her new property and baby updates.' If that is your version of success, then by all means it's a lovely conversation to have. But if you feel triggered or confused by why those things don't light you up, and your version of success is different to this, it may feel like you have to constantly justify yourself.

It's been seven years since Olivia moved on from a big job in the City which was making her miserable, and yet she says, 'I'm still asked why I would walk away from the legal profession, why I would halve my salary. I'm asked why I rent – rather than buy a house, whether I'm dating. Celebrating successes which are otherwise the "norm" does become difficult when you must explain and defend them.'

It forces us to look in the mirror and realize we have to fight for our own version of success. To stand up for it, protect it, and be proud of it like it's our own baby. When I asked what Olivia's version of success is now, after a relationship break-down and changing jobs, she said, 'Now it's about work-life balance: authenticity, friendships, health and contentment matter more to me than box ticking.'

I have a friend who has been avoiding going to weddings, as she finds the 'What do you do?' questions really tricky, and they ultimately make her feel bad about herself. Missing out makes her feel guilty, but she struggles to voice her own defin-ition of success, or indeed let people know she's still working it out, when she's seemingly the only single person who is looking for a new job. Like Olivia, sometimes we feel like we have to defend our own version of success, especially when we feel outnumbered. But instead of focusing only on what our online lives look like or have to offer, it's about digging deep and acknowledging where we are right now. If we can continue to ask ourselves what we are really aiming for, away from beautiful pictures on the internet, we can stay aligned with our own personal goals, stay in our lane, and stay on our own side, even when we feel alienated. Everything feels easier when we can find a way to be our own friend during these moments. Sometimes that can mean taking a break from other people's success stories online or in real life. It can also mean realizing that you don't have to hide away just because your life looks different to others'. We should do whatever it takes to find compassion for ourselves. Every path is different, and we are each moving at our own speed.

Myth: We're Missing Out by Not Joining In

FOMO (fear of missing out) is real. We all have that one thing we privately worry about on a quiet Sunday evening: '*I'm not very good at my job*', '*I'll never meet the right person*', '*I should do more exercise*', or whatever happens to pop up, unwelcome, in our brains at any given time. I sometimes worry I'm not very fun. 'Fun' is everywhere. 'Fun' is marketed to us 24/7. Everyone is having *fun* on Instagram. Fun at festivals, fun at parties, fun in the sun! Female TV show protagonists are often fun, wild and adventurous. Drinking culture is about squeezing in the most amount of fun. Yesterday I noticed a book in the window of Waterstones called *The Power of Fun*. We buy the T-shirts that say 'Life Is Short'. We use the hashtag #yolo. We are meant to be making the most of every single moment of our short lives.

But if someone asked me, in all seriousness, what my ideal evening would consist of, I would close my eyes and think of the following (in this order):

1. Soaking myself in a bath full of salts and oils until I wrinkle like a prune.

2. Lying horizontal underneath a big blanket wearing thick socks.

3. Propping myself up with an oversized pillow.

4. Settling into a good, solid book (hardback, not on Kindle).

5. Getting an early night.

I know what you're thinking: this reminds you of the sort of evening someone's grandma would have. Yet it's my personal version of a successful evening. For someone else it might mean a big night out, or a concert, or night-time surfing. We each have our favourite ways to spend our time.

Last summer I went on a trip to Ibiza, on my own. I was writing a feature about 'holidaying solo'. On the second day I received a text from a friend:

Friend: How is it!! What have you been doing??

I was in bed, wrapped in a towel, writing my article while eating a salad and listening to Fleetwood Mac. The night before I'd had dinner on my own before heading to bed by nine p.m.

Me: I'm writing in bed, staying in again tonight. Bliss!
Friend: You're staying IN? You're in IBIZA? Go out and go to a rave. If I was there, I'd drag you out, at least for a bit. Go on, you should go to one of the parties!
Me: I'm having the best time here, in my room, reading!
Friend: Lol. This trip is wasted on you!

Although she was (partly) joking, and she didn't mean any harm, there is a quiet expectation that in your twenties and thirties you shouldn't be boring. This friend would have probably gone and bought some drugs and let her hair down and partied all night. Whereas I would almost always choose to stay in.

Of course, I have privileges at home most of the time. Being in a couple means that I always have the option to have company and I don't feel lonely at home. I have space and I can host my friends comfortably. The reality is that I just really like being at home. I was in my element last New Year's Eve – I had my friends round, cooked dinner, then was able to sneak off to bed while everyone else carried on partying until the sun came up the next day. I struggle to stay up late, and it feels good to set your own boundaries and not always ignore or push past what you're comfortable with. Since the pandemic, people like to say you should get out of your house at any opportunity and seize the day. But that's not the only definition of seizing the day.

Maybe after years of thinking I wanted a Big Crazy Life, I just want a Quieter Life, spending time with the people I love without ruining my shoes on a sticky dance floor in the process. I'm done with hangovers; I'm done with going along with other people's definition of fun. I am exploring my own version, which may look quieter than others'. I do sometimes have moments when I worry that I will look back at my younger years and regret not being more 'wild'. But then again, I remind myself that forced fun is not the same as proper fun, that being wild was never my desire. We need to work out what fun means for us, rather than following the crowd, however uncomfortable that might feel.

On a recent episode of *Desert Island Discs*, even Kate Moss admitted she is no longer her party-girl self, that she likes an early night, her garden and not being 'out of control'. If it's good enough for Kate, it's good enough for me.

Myth: We Should Have Lots of Friends

A few years ago, I met Gillian Anderson and interviewed her for my podcast *Ctrl Alt Delete*. She is the coolest, smartest, most down-to-earth woman imaginable. We had a photo taken together afterwards, snuggled inside the recording booth, and she was warm and friendly. I remember us talking about her career, her life, her charity work, her habits, her hopes, and then, at the end of the conversation, I asked her about her thoughts on friendship. I had recently read an interview with her in the *Guardian* where she said something quite rare about friendship. She said she only had a few friends, explaining that she celebrated her fifty-first birthday with three small parties, in London, in Canada and in the US. 'But it was only five people, six, and 13,' she says, merrily. 'Those are all the friends I have [. . .] I don't have hundreds of people in my life. I don't have 300 people to invite.' Hearing someone (who I can't help but slightly idolize) say this, made me feel instantly less alone. I only have a few friends too! We spoke about really leaning into your own joy and she encouraged my listeners to do this 'at any age'. We don't have to wait until we are older or wiser to do things that work for us; we can push back on the 'shoulds' and decide how we'd like to live. There is a lot of pressure on young people to be popular, but hearing Gillian Anderson admit she was happy with a handful of good friends, and not a huge squad, made my shoulders relax. Her evenings sounded similar to mine.

I've always been fascinated by how friendships play such a

variety of roles in different people's lives. My sister, for example, has lots of friends. For her thirtieth birthday, I organized a little book of memories for her. My inbox was pinging every two seconds with new messages, and some of them were too long to physically fit inside. She has so many good friends who know her so well and it was beautiful to see. But I couldn't help but compare my friendships, and I felt like I didn't have such an abundance. I can count the people I feel genuinely close to on one hand, or maybe two at a push. I don't have a huge squad of besties, but I have strong individual relationships with people. I'm better one-on-one, and have always found it hard to maintain strong relationships being part of a big group.

I'm not sure where my insecurity came from. Maybe it was seeing that photo of Taylor Swift's star-studded 'girl squad' of friends at the VMAs (MTV Video Music Awards). Or those photos of twenty-two women on a hen-do or group holiday. I have realized that deep down there is perhaps a fear of being alone or simply a need for more validation. By having more of it, we may then feel more accepted or move loved. But according to research conducted in 2016 by MIT (Massachusetts Institute of Technology), we don't need tons of friends to feel fulfilled. Our capacity for simultaneous close friendships peaks at approximately five people. Even though social media encourages us to constantly make 'friends' with people, in real life we simply don't have the room.

It takes a lot of work to maintain the friendships we do have. As entrepreneur Chelsea Fagan said on Twitter: 'There's a lot of importance placed on the "work" of maintaining romantic relationships, but very little about how the same directed, intentional care needs to go towards real friendships. We're not honest about the fact that you can only afford to really do it for a few people.' But I'd say that this intentional work is well worth it, thanks to the rewards it reaps. As with all the best things in life, we have to work hard to maintain the things we love – we have to call the friend, do the work, leave the house, show up. Digital mindfulness expert Christina Crook calls these ways to cultivate happiness 'good burdens'. It's not easy, it's effortful, but that's the whole point. It's the doing that makes it all worthwhile.

You don't need a massive group of friends if that hasn't happened to you or isn't something you necessarily need or want. But friendship is important, and warm relationships are such a valuable part of life. Our digital culture tells us that everything is a numbers game. That we should have hundreds of friends. A million followers. That life is a popularity contest. In reality, a small number of warm friendships can give you a lifetime of happiness: quality over quantity.

Myth: Success Means Finding a Partner, and Sticking with Them for Ever

On Twitter, writer and activist Jamie Klingler posted, 'Who are these actual adults [. . .] who believe they need someone to fix them, complete them, make them whole. Fuck that. Be a fully formed human that is enhanced by connections and relationships. Not completed. You aren't half.' I am surrounded by women in my life who enjoy being single, are complete just as themselves, and live full lives on their own. But despite there being many outwardly happy single women, there is still a lingering taboo about singledom. The idea of being lonely, or alone, or left on a shelf permeates pop culture narratives. As writer Dolly Alderton says, there is often a 'premium placed on romantic love culturally'. 'Cuffing season' is a term rising in popularity, referring to a specific period in the calendar year when, apparently, people feel more motivated to get 'coupled up'. It generally occurs from October to March, i.e. the colder parts of the year in the UK, and especially during the holiday season between Christmas and New Year. It suggests a want or need for company during these periods, but much of it is driven by a social pressure to bring a plus-one to a holiday party, or to have a relationship to discuss with family over the Christmas turkey. In my experience, people seem to ask single people lots of questions, wanting to know if they really like it, or if they just 'haven't met the right person yet', quizzing them in a different way to other people who are coupled up. Like with being childfree, it seems to be one of those things that people feel is up for discussion, when it really isn't. There is a longstanding societal pressure to get married or have a relationship and it's everywhere.

Even when in a relationship, we can celebrate alone time. I've personally never felt the need to be joined to a partner at the hip. When I first met my husband, Paul, we were very happily single. I know it sounds clichéd, but neither of us was really looking for a partner, so we were able to meet each other without any sense of desperation, and to quite casually get to know each other. It helped that we were in our early twenties; it's a whole different ball game when you're older because you need to ask the bigger questions sooner. He would go away for five weeks at a time on photography trips, and I was actually quite happy to have the bed to myself and some alone time to do as I liked and feel independent. Of course I missed him, but I didn't want to feel like we were each other's 'halves'; I already felt whole in myself. I didn't want to lose that. I love alone time. I love being my own person and having my own identity outside of a long-term relationship.

Paul and I have been lucky to grow together in the same way, but even so, people's life expectancy is getting longer, and the idea that we will definitely stay married to the same person for ever is not a given. Marriage is a huge commitment, and it's not something to go into lightly. It's not about expecting it *not* to work out, there should be a strong intention to stay together, but a relationship shouldn't be a trap either, if things change beyond our control.

We've seen that it's totally natural for our ambition to wax and wane throughout our lives, and sometimes this can bring about change in our relationships too. We are in a *constant* state of flux and change. In many ways it is down to luck if you both grow together in the same way. As Esther Perel claims, 'I've had three marriages with the same husband.' When I interviewed her on *Ctrl Alt Delete*, she said that you can have many different relationships within the same partnership, because we all grow, and change, and we either grow together or grow apart, but nothing stays the same. You essentially keep committing to the same person over and over again – or you don't. This recommitting by choice is the romantic side of marriage: choosing to stay together, choosing to keep going. You either grow together like tree roots wrapping around each other, or grow apart and end up going your separate ways. Of course, if you do grow apart, it's a very difficult thing to go through, but we shouldn't see relationships that didn't last as 'wasted time' if you break up or get divorced. It's not like a whole meaningful chapter of your life has been erased, just because it's ended. I remember hearing an anecdote about a woman telling someone she was going through a divorce, and they replied, 'Congratulations'. She said she loved that response, because that's how it felt; it did feel like something to be congratulated for.

Myth: We Should All Want to Start a Family

A photo of a friend's new baby lights up a Whatsapp group on a Tuesday afternoon, with her tiny wrinkly hands, eyes squeezed tight shut, wearing a little hat. Someone in the group commented, 'All babies look the same to me! But this one is V CUTE.' I posted a row of cry-laughing emojis at the honesty of the comment, followed by heart emojis at the cuteness of the picture.

A friend's toddler 'wished' me a happy birthday last week, lying in front of a whiteboard on which her mother had scrawled a message.

A friend's son sang 'Happy BIRFday EMMA' while punching the sofa and chewing a soft toy.

Another friend's toddler picked up a guitar bigger than

him, looking so lost in the music (noise) he was making, it reminded me of the purest moments of creativity.

My daredevil nephew throws himself down muddy, grassy hills on his bike, this tiny little guy living life on the edge with the wind in his hair, not afraid of anything. I'm surrounded by children that aren't my own. For me, children are a reminder that when you strip away all the many layers of cultural conditioning of adult life, things can be pretty simple. I love these children in my life.

I might be only seeing a highlight reel of the good bits, but I'm seeing them for what they truly are: moments of genuine, unfiltered joy. Children naturally believe in equality, they furrow their brows with concern when an adult pretends to cry; they randomly kiss you on the elbow and then run away; they do what they want, they go after what they want. I love their essence, their energy, their often-bonkers personalities. We should take a leaf out of their book.

And yet, however much I love other people's kids, this does not, even for a moment, translate into me wanting my own. And hey – it turns out these two facts can absolutely exist together. I have never wanted children. In the summer of 2020, when my debut novel *OLIVE* was first published, I accidentally-on-purpose became a voice on the topic of choosing to be childfree. Olive is a childfree-by-choice protagonist. I knew that writing a topical novel would put me in the firing line for questions about it, as we can't help but think a female novelist must be writing about her personal life. And to be fair, this time I was. Although I made sure that I was nothing like Olive physically or emotionally, without really meaning to, I became a top Google search, a SEO hit for 'childfree by choice woman'. I wrote about it for *ELLE*, *Grazia*, *Marie Claire*, BBC *Woman's Hour* and more. I've felt emotionally exposed and vulnerable at times, peeling back a layer of my life, but mostly I've been loving the open-hearted, like-minded emails I've received off the back of people's late-night internet searches. I love the twists and turns and nuance of the conversation, how it always goes back to having compassion for each other's personal choices and desires. I feel it as much in my bones that I don't want children as another woman who absolutely knows she does. I am grateful that I can even have this conversation. The documentary film *My So-Called Selfish Life* shows how women in the 1970s were ostracized for committing the biggest sin: not wanting to use their bodies to procreate. They were fired from jobs, disowned by family members and made to feel like complete pariahs.

While some people still see childfree life as a moral failing – which of course is completely untrue, and especially unfair on those who can't have children – thankfully things are somewhat better today. But a taboo still lingers if you say, 'I don't want kids.' I always feel the need to quickly follow up with 'But I still love them!', or 'I love being an auntie!', or 'But I am a really CARING person!' The real breakthrough will be when someone doesn't need to follow up with anything *at all* and for that to be completely fine. A gentle smile and a 'good for you' will suffice.

One thing I really enjoy, being childfree, is being a safe space for my friends who are parents. Even though I am not a parent and can't really understand what they go through or experience day to day, I am a judgement-free zone. In many ways it's brought me closer to my friends with kids, not pulled us apart. I had a conversation with a friend recently and we were reflecting on what we've all been through during the pandemic. She's self-employed and is used to designing her life her own way. Suddenly, the extra pressure of home-schooling was sucking away time, energy and resources. I felt the opposite in many ways, as though I had nothing taking me away from my work during lockdowns. She had too much distraction, I had not enough distraction. I didn't have another part of my life to tend to. I didn't have a child tugging at my sleeve, pulling me out of my own head or putting a deadline on my work. All I did was work. From her position, she would have loved some more free time: more time to get her work done. I would have loved someone to come into my office and immediately demand to play or distract me. In that moment, we both wanted a bit more of what the other person had. We'd idealized each other's situation, which happens so much in life. The conversation weirdly made each of us feel better.

In his *The School of Life* video called 'To Have or Not to Have Children', Alain De Botton's soothing voice explains that there's no such thing as a 'cost-free' decision. No matter what your life looks like, there will be downsides, sunken costs and moments where the grass seems as though it could be so much greener. He says it's all about choosing your own specific type of suffering (I love his intense choice of words). Whether you have kids or not, whether you got to choose or not: suffering comes for us all at some point. It's just differently branded, in a differently shaped tin. That's not meant to sound depressing but comforting in its universality. All we can do is support each other as best we can. Because, nestled amongst our own specific types of joy is our own specific type of suffering, something we all have in common. Realizing that we are all on a separate journey doesn't mean we're alone, but it does mean we have to make decisions that are right for *us*. No one else has the map, only we do.

Myth: Just Buy a Few Less Avocados

In 2017, Australian real-estate mogul Tim Gurner told millennials to stop eating avocado on toast and put the money they'd saved towards a house instead. Millennials had long been associated with the popular brunch meal for some reason, and this really doubled down on the stereotype: solve your housing woes by having fewer expensive breakfasts with friends. Of course, then came the sarcastic social media posts and memes. Jennifer Albright tweeted, 'I was gonna put a downpayment on a house last year but then I spent $44,000 on avocado toast.' She's being flippant, but it's not right to put the onus on individuals, when the whole system is unsupportive. It's like telling millennials to stop buying houseplants, to help solve a global climate crisis.

It's harder than ever to buy your first house, to earn enough money for kids, to save up for a nice car, so why not spend your hard-earned cash on a few nice brunches rather than squirrelling it away for some fruitless goal? Of course, most things in life seem to be about balance, but we shouldn't beat ourselves up over having the odd treat or thing that lifts us out of a funk. As I've outlined in previous chapters, 'success' in these areas is not as easy as 1-2-3 when we still have systemic issues at play, namely a lack of equal opportunity in society, which means many are denied the chance to thrive. As marketing and publicity director Polly Osborn said on Twitter, 'For anyone who needs to hear it: it's totally ok to not own a house and have a good time in your 20s living somewhere you want to live. I bought my first property at 38 and yes, yes, yes, I could have lived off beans and lived in the arse end of nowhere but what for?' Why not spend your money on exactly what you like, on your own personal tickboxes?

Myth: Only the Traditional Milestones Are Worth Celebrating

A friend of mine is single and lives on her own in a beautiful house with a dog. She is godmother to many of her friends' children and a really great friend, somebody who shows up for people around her: she remembers birthdays, organizes parties, sends thoughtful texts. In a world of endless celebrations around relationships – engagements, hen dos, weddings, baby showers – how do we make sure people not taking part in these things are also celebrated? We discussed the idea of a big birthday party – a self-celebration party. A chance for friends and family to show up and demonstrate their love.

I'd love for this idea to be normalized. To throw a 'just because' party, without needing to have a textbook life-milestone to hang it on. We also discussed ways in which she should celebrate herself, treat herself, feel like she is also appreciating and seeing her own value, even if others are tied up elsewhere. It doesn't seem fair, does it, that mile-stone celebrations seem to always be around marriage and babies, and require the forking out of endless cash for these occasions? There are so many other things we could and should celebrate. We are all worthy of celebrating, regard-less of whether or not there's a Clintons card for it. These classic cultural markers are not the only sign of success.

Chapter Reflections

I. **Ask yourself: Is it true?** Write down something that is troubling you. Some thoughts are so embedded, that we never ever question them. Write down a few things that make you feel as though you're not achieving what everyone else is. For example, 'I don't have enough friends.' See if you can switch it around and write down anything that comes to mind. Name one friend, new or old, who you appreciate. What is it exactly that is making you feel as though you should have more?

2. **Are you holding on to any 'shoulds'?** What 'shoulds' in your life feel embedded from your upbringing? Were you brought up thinking you should have a certain thing by a certain age? You 'should' get married? You 'should' get a PhD? Make two columns on a piece of paper: on one side write down your 'should', and on the other side write the things that bring you joy. Which ones match up? Which differences do you spot?

3. **Celebrate others' alternative milestones:** Going to therapy. Getting a dog. Going through a divorce. Make them feel seen and supported in the same way we would if they were reaching a traditional tick-list moment. Go for a coffee, send a text message, post a card, or organize a small gathering.

4. **Have compassion for yourself, like a friend.** What would you say to a friend who hasn't quite reached a certain goal yet? You'd be kind and supportive. Offer that same tone to yourself during moments when you are yearning for

something in particular. Write a note to your past
self telling them all the good things they would
never have seen coming. Write to your future self
too, listing all the things you hope they will have
one day. Put these notes in a drawer and focus on
today by doing something kind for yourself. It's
all a work in progress.

The Arrival Myth

'I'm not willing to spend my life racing to the top
of the mountain because I've learnt that when I let
myself pause for long enough, the view is glorious
from exactly where I stand.'

NICOLA JANE HOBBS

The other day, I woke up in a good mood, having gone out
to a restaurant for a delicious meal with friends the night
before and laughed until my belly hurt. Standing in the kitchen, I spread lashings of butter across a hot cross bun and
told Google Home to play Magic FM. The song that blasted
out was Earth, Wind & Fire's 'Let's Groove' and my mind
flashed back to the photoshoot for my first book. This song
was playing on an eighties' playlist while I was posing for the
photos that would end up on the cover. It was the ultimate

dream, the success I'd wished for: a make-up artist from *Strictly Come Dancing* was painting my lips red, my editor was telling me how excited she was about the book, her assistant was laying out coffees and snacks, and my photographer friend was taking the photos, laughing with me in between outfit changes. I couldn't believe it. A photoshoot. For my first book. I felt on top of the world. I had done it. My life was going to change for ever. This was IT. The arrival.

However, a few months after the book came out, I went to a press event and made small talk with loads of people from the industry there. 'How's everything going?' 'OMG your book!' 'Smashing it!' 'You must be so happy having a book out!' 'You're doing soooo well!' Then, I bumped into my friend Kate Leaver, a warm soul and a fellow writer, and seeing her kind face made me break down the facade. I pulled her to one side and told her I felt completely deflated. I was embarrassed to say it. It felt so anticlimactic. The book coming out didn't make me feel much different at all. It didn't help that the early sales weren't great either. Kate was really understanding, but I could tell she was also a little surprised. My life really did look pretty perfect on the outside. I felt strange and alone. And I felt guilty for complaining. But I was so disappointed. My childhood dream had happened, and yet, I felt the same inside as I did before.

My Arrival, So I Thought

This common phenomenon is a psychological thought trap called 'arrival fallacy', a term coined by Tal Ben-Shahar, the Harvard psychology expert. This fallacy is the 'illusion that once we make it, once we attain our goal or reach our destination, we will reach lasting happiness'. If you are someone who has never felt totally fulfilled, even if, on paper, you've ticked a fair bit off your life-goal list, then it might be down to this. There is an assumption that once we reach a big life or career goal, we will finally be version 2.0 and we will stay there. You will feel different, better. Then the disappointment sets in. We realize the fictional 'destination' doesn't exist.

I now understand that the anticlimax after achieving a dream milestone is completely normal, but the problem is that a) the moment hardly ever matches up to how we think it'll feel, and b) we don't really talk about it. According to clinical psychologist Dr Sophie Mort, there are many reasons why this anticlimax happens, including that 'When we aim for a milestone, we often have lots of structure in our day [. . .] when we cross the finish line we expect to feel elated, however, we can suddenly feel lost as we don't exactly know what to do with our time any more.' She also mentions that if we are perfectionists, we can feel that we should have done better, often imagining that we will feel 'like a different person' once we achieve our goals, but 'realize that we are still the same person who still has all the same worries'. This leads ultimately to a deep sense of disappointment and the reasons behind it are often hard to place.

Just because you're succeeding in one area, it doesn't mean you're succeeding in all areas, and life can continue to be hard and painful once you achieve a goal. I am guilty of looking at Hollywood stars and being completely distracted by the make-up, the sequins and the lights, without stopping to think about the full picture. I really do try and remind myself of the quote, 'Everyone is fighting a battle you know nothing about.' When I spoke to Laura, who shared with me her experience of achieving her dream of publishing her first book (at the age of fifty), she said other areas of her life started crumbling away.

Within that same week, she very sadly lost a parent and her home. The success of the book did not make every other issue magically disappear: 'It could not act as the cure-all or shield for which I had subconsciously been hoping.' There is always the undercurrent of everyday life bubbling away, whether we realize our dreams or we don't. There is work to be done underneath, and no amount of surface-level success can ever paper over the cracks. She added, 'You get the dream job or meet the dream partner or have the baby or write the book or get the starring role or get the acceptance letter or win the lottery, but at the end of the day, you're still you; you still have the same wounds and childhood traumas that need healing, you're still human, you can still get sick, you can still lose a parent or a job or a partner.' Success in one aspect does not mean success in all aspects, nor does it mean the end of the story.

The glitz and glamour of S.U.C.C.E.S.S in shiny bright lights is not something you can hang your life on, nor does it last. As science professor Adam Grant says: 'Success is a temporary thrill. Happiness lies in doing daily activities that bring you joy.' The reason I went into a black hole of anticlimactic disappointment after my book came out is not because anything was wrong, but because my *expectations* were all wrong. I had been sold a pill that didn't work. Success is a brand that we buy into. A marketing tool to keep us chasing, keep us on our toes, never content. I look back now and cringe at myself for thinking that doing well at work would be the solution to all my problems.

Listening to that Earth, Wind & Fire song in my kitchen made me smile because it was also a reminder that I've come so far. I'm no longer a twenty-something having her photo taken, thinking that a book or a goal or an achievement will change her life. I'm now in my thirties, having achieved some stuff I'm proud of, doing a job I love, but this time I'm wearing Crocs (sorry), slowing down slightly, taking time to smell the roses, appreciating where I'm at and realizing that the shiny end-goal isn't the main piece of the puzzle any more. Sure, I still have achievements and goals on my bucket list, which can be a cherry on top and make me feel good, but it's the framework I now have around me that actually makes my life meaningful and joyous. I have the ability to zoom out and see my self-worth, regardless of what I've 'achieved' that day. Through unpicking the success myths, you, too, should feel empowered to create your own frame-work which acknowledges that achievements are an added bonus to a life that already feels good in so many other ways, and are not the be-all and end-all. Underneath it all, you are already enough, and you get to decide what a successful life looks like.

'Success' now is in the minutiae of the way I spend my days. It's committing to doing things that help myself and others. It's showing up. It's taking care of myself. It's paying the bills without losing my mind. Or having a long walk. Or calling a friend. Or having a new adventure. Or meeting my deadline. Or being brave. Or saying no. Or having a lie down. I don't need someone from *Strictly Come Dancing* to do my make-up to make me feel valid. I just need to be me. When we unpick the myths, we open ourselves up to a new-found sense of freedom and get to design our lives from scratch.

Throughout this book we've seen how our desire to crack the success formula, and our obsession with happiness, productivity, status, money and our work identity (as well as society's insistence on a traditional set of tickboxes), leaves us feeling frustrated and empty. The arrival myth sums up all of that fruitless striving. The thing is, with 'more' it never stops. So, nothing's ever good enough. A couple I know recently bought a massive six-bedroom dream house on Rightmove, the deal had just gone through. When I recently saw them, one of them had a Rightmove alert pop up on her phone. She didn't want to delete the app, saying she wanted to keep the alerts just in case a better house came up in the future. She was already plotting their next move! She laughed and knew it was ridiculous, but it proved the point that so many of us can't quite feel satisfied with what we've got in the moment, even if it would have once been beyond our wildest dreams.

Chasing Our Own Montage Moment

Montage scenes in feel-good films are uplifting to watch, but it's worth remembering that they're not very realistic. One of my favourites has always been Elle Woods's 'making it' moment in *Legally Blonde*. She's on the exercise bike, she's hustling hard at work, she's surrounded by books, she's going to prove everyone wrong. It's such a great scene, and we all want to be her. Except, in real life her hard work wouldn't stop once she'd won the trial. A new challenge would await, and the cycle would continue. She has to get up and go again. Her life continues, and there will be other struggles. We often assume our life is full of those big montage moments and then the credits roll: *Fin*.

We cannot jump ahead, or fast-forward to the good bits, or delete the bad scenes, as much as we might want to. In her newsletter, LA-based freelance writer Heather Sundell wrote, 'Can't I just cut to the good part? When the kitchen is done. When she sleeps through the night. When he's finally potty trained. When schools stop closing because of Covid. When I get my degree. When I can go on a vacation with my husband again – let alone a dinner.' A lot of enjoying life in the moment is about patience, and the ability to be OK with where we are right now. A bit like watching a film the whole way through. As Heather reflects: '"the good part" is an urban legend. It doesn't exist – on its own at least. The next phase will bring its own seasonal storms, and the life I'm currently living is the good part too, even if I cruelly won't be able to see or feel it for years.' The mundane bits of life *are* often the good parts too, we just don't see it at the time.

When I was younger, I was convinced that certain moments would have the power to transform me. Like in a classic montage clip with background music, I believed I could, overnight, become a better version of myself with a few minor life changes. It started with the smallest (and saddest) of goals: upgrading my iPod; feng shui-ing my bedroom; winning a race. Everything was an opportunity for a portal to open and for a 'new me' to come out on the other side. When I reached [insert particular goal] or got [insert particular thing], I believed everything would finally fall into place. It might sound silly, but my first memory of feeling as though I may 'arrive' somewhere better through an external factor was on a trip to the shops to buy a new school uniform. I picked up a grey skirt which was pleated and short, instead of long and straight, and I tried on some new school shoes with a slight heel. I was going to be a different person once I put them on. I just knew it. But when I looked in the mirror at my new outfit, I realized I was still me. I still had the same problems and still had to do my homework. You don't shapeshift overnight just because you get a promotion, a new home or a new pair of shoes.

We grow up with linear thinking. Beginning, middle and end. But in reality, our lives are cyclical. We go round and round in stages, growing and changing all the time. We go in and out like the magnetic push and pull of ocean tides, moving in rhythms. The beginning of our lives is much like the end: we care for elderly family members as though they are children, just as they washed and cared for us. It is a circle of life; we don't arrive anywhere – we end up where we began. We pass on our skills and knowledge to the next generation. Over the course of your life, you will 'arrive' over and over again (a new relationship, a new career, this or that) but you won't stay there. Human beings are always evolving, we never stay the same, so our definitions of success for ourselves should always change too.

Don't Let Your Dreams Ruin Your Life

In 2018 I had a successful year, on paper, but I kept moving the goalposts to bigger things, despite achieving many things on my career list. *I must not be trying hard enough*, I thought! Despite meeting the Queen as part of the Queen's Young Leaders Award, hitting twelve million downloads of my podcast and doing a Ted Talk, none of it felt how I thought it would. Surely these goals were big enough, so why weren't they fulfilling me? I was confused. I was supposed to be on cloud nine. I was so busy that I wasn't savouring any of it and I couldn't properly take it all in because it was a whirl-wind. Before I could catch my breath, I was always on to the next thing. I was flown to Hollywood to be in a TV advert, but I don't remember much of it because I was already thinking, *What will be next? How can I sustain this? Why don't I feel good?*

Everything in my life had become increasingly goal orientated – to the point where I'd start putting things off because I believed my life would only truly 'start' after reaching said goal. I would procrastinate about things like inviting friends round, exercising more, booking that trip, because the timing never felt right, and I never quite felt ready. I wasn't the person I wanted to be yet. I was waiting for some-thing. *When* I get that job, *when* I am older, *when* I move to London, *when* I go on that diet, *when* I have enough money . . . When, when, when. I was working hard, but I was always, always living in the future.

It's an unfortunate thing to look back and realize how much of life you might have put on pause because you were too busy striving for the 'when' moments. Society has us believe that if we keep moving ourselves up a ladder, we will reach a point of eternal happiness. It's designed to keep us all on the conveyor belt of never feeling satisfied.

I remember giving this arrival tactic one last go. I decided I would pick a huge challenge and see if then I would finally, eventually 'arrive'. So, then I thought, *I'll write a novel*. When I write a novel, THEN it'll all click into place. Then I'll be happy. And now, two years on from publishing that novel, I am back at square one again. I did not arrive. There is no such thing as arrival, but the idea of it keeps us trying desperately to sustain the success we have, and keeps us constantly chasing for more. As I've said, there's nothing wrong with chasing – the chase can be enjoyable – but there is nothing that different waiting for you on the other side. Change how you feel now, right now, and then you are actually truly changing your life. We need to accept the reality of our own present moment.

If someone had told me these things before I [insert dream goal] though, I would have felt very dispirited: *What do you mean your whole life doesn't miraculously change overnight? Why do anything at all if we don't feel totally changed afterwards?* It was only when I read the phrase, 'Sometimes wanting something is better than having it', on Mark Manson's website that it clicked for me, although it took me a few minutes of contemplation to come around to this idea. *Wanting* is better than *having*? Really? I've definitely experienced my imagination, daydreams and fantasies often being better than the end reality. My memories of striving to get published are more alive in my mind than the day I got the book deal. Our imagination is limitless. Think about the thrill of the search for something new. That feeling just before you're ready to make a change. The feeling of knowing you're about to fall in love. When we have things, they can disappoint us or not measure up; it is impossible to expect any human being to perfectly match our ideal standards, and we shouldn't expect that level of fantasy perfection from our lives either. Arriving is only disappointing when we had imagined something different. Arriving doesn't exist, because our lives don't come in clear-cut chapters; instead they are a long, continuous line of things.

Farrah Storr wrote recently on her Substack, *Things Worth Knowing*, about how her definition of success has drastically changed, and described it beautifully: 'When I think about success, I always think about Philip Larkin's most brilliant phrase "fulfilment's desolate attic". Because that's what conventional success can ultimately feel like. It's certainly something I found when I got to the top of editing magazines. It was all rather empty: a penthouse with few balloons. When I got to the top I looked back over my career and realized the joy was in the climb to the top, not the pinnacle. If success then is in the climb, for me success is smaller things nowadays, mulching the flower beds ready for spring, putting up boxes before the birds hatch, writing a few lines of prose every single day.' Everywhere I look, ambitious women are making peace with this fact: the joy was in the climb.

Now that I've fully embraced this truth, it's been liberating to realize that I will never 'arrive' and that all the obvious outward achievements will perhaps never provide the feeling of having 'made it'. As the novelist Cheryl Strayed said: 'Don't let your dreams ruin your life.' I find it strangely uplifting. I wanted to write this book to celebrate lifting ourselves up and figuring out our own paths to success, freeing ourselves from the set-in-stone culture of only focusing on the top of the mountain. It isn't about striving for less or having fewer career goals – it's more about realizing that there probably won't be a big, life-changing, *Stars In Their Eyes* moment at the end of it all. Life will be the same. Or a bit more comfortable materially. But 'success' will not give you a miraculous transition or graduation or stepping stone to a different you. So, it's more beneficial in the long run to stop strategically planning the 'when' moments and live for the now.

It's Time for Phase Two

So, how do you get to a place where you can be as comfortable in the doing as the achieving? It's hard to go against what we're used to, and many of us feel guilty admitting, 'actually, something's not quite right' when other people are clapping at your external markers of success. Most self-help books try and neatly tie a bow on everything, promising you ten steps to success, inspiring you to follow your dreams and never have any problems again. I am still susceptible to these messages, and then kick myself when another $300 course from an online guru doesn't fix all my life problems. It feels almost impossible to definitively conclude a book that is all about figuring out your own definition of success. Understanding your own version of success takes a lot of work. It really is different for all of us. It starts with putting down all the forms of escapism that we use daily, even for a moment, so we can sit quietly in a room with our own thoughts, which can be terrifying for a lot of us. But without truly trying to figure out what we want (rather than what our friends, partner, family, or even someone on Instagram wants) we will just blindly go along with what everyone else is telling us to do, living somebody else's dream. We will continue to be a circle trying to fit into a square all our lives, wondering why we remain unhappy and stuck, no matter how many bells and whistles we acquire along the way. We don't need a map; we need to strip things away occasionally and remind ourselves that we are each our own compass. The question to ask yourself is simple, but hard: *What do I want?*

I cryptically mentioned my arrival at phase two in the Ambition Myth chapter, something that was first explained to me by author and coach Donna Lancaster, who wrote *The Bridge*. We need to go through 'Phase one' (i.e. the path we think we want) in order to get to 'Phase two', which is a path of inner contentment and happiness. Phase one is really important. We all have to get things wrong, take different turns, and want what we *think* we want, first. None of our lives or journeys are ever wasted, because phase one is crucial. It's only through phase one that we get to phase two.

Phase one: a pursuit of society's traditional definition of success (extrinsic goals, status, material wealth, etc.).
Phase two: unlearning phase one and finding your inner contentment that does not solely come from the pursuit of 'more'.

Lancaster explains, 'Phase one is a necessary phase, it's the job, the money, the partner, the shoes . . . whatever it might be. You're acquiring those to get a sense of your self. As you move into phase two (and it happens at different stages, and some people never leave phase one), where you redefine that definition of success that has nothing to do with career and money, you go inside out. You arrive at this place where you see life through a very different set of lenses. You start to see the different kinds of riches that are available to us, and none of them relate to pound signs – not that there's anything wrong with money.' Some people spend all their life in phase one, trying to fix their life by adding more on. Some people go into phase two a lot earlier, such as teenagers who follow their inner compass from the outset. Some people go into phase two after their working life is over. We are all different, all at different stages, all in different phases. The main thing is that phase one is necessary, because we learn so much from it. There is no such thing as a 'wrong' path because all of life's moments have the potential to teach us something. Everything in this book is designed to help you work out your inner feelings and desires, and work towards (or through) phase two. Phase two is when your original definition of success no longer works for you, and you are looking for something deeper and less obvious. Curiosity is leading the way more than desire or hunger. Success isn't where progress stops, it is normally where it begins as we realize there is more self-growth to do beyond the material things we gain.

If we find our truest path by discovering what *doesn't* make us happy, by experiencing the fallacy for ourselves, we also need to be open to the lessons it's telling us. During those moments where you feel disappointed that you haven't arrived (again), make a mental note of the feeling, write down what is still missing, be aware of this moment. Sit with it. The key is to stop jumping right back on the treadmill and doing it all over again. There is a moment to learn and grow in absolutely everything.

Success used to mean never-ending wealth.
Success can now mean time wealth.

Success used to mean constant busyness.
Success can now mean resting.

Success used to mean always striving.
Success can now mean knowing what enough feels like.

I hope it's been helpful to see how ditching the rigid traditional definitions of success reveals the many different ways we can find fulfilment in our lives. I've found it fascinating speaking to people about their distinct versions of success and realizing we are all so different: some people think loving your job too much means you have failed; some people think it's a shame to settle down with no passions; some people think it's the biggest success to thrive and be alone; some think it's marrying the person of your dreams. Some women I know think success is being selfish with your life, and some think it's adopting eight kids. There is no one answer. There never was, and never will be. We have to stop policing other people's versions of success – your path to success is a solo journey.

Crucially, if you're reading this book and feel as though you've 'failed' in any way, remember that all those wrong turns or moments of 'this isn't right' are *helpful* in discovering what we want. It's like a game of hot-or-cold: are you getting warmer? Are you getting colder? We need to know what *doesn't* make us feel successful, in order to figure out what does. No one gets to work out the puzzle without taking a few wrong steps first.

Validation and Values

It's hard to make the shift between phases and it is not a quick process. It can take time to transition, to find ourselves, to work things out. We go through so many big changes in our lives, and countless micro-changes too. My previous relationship with success was tangled up with lots of guilt and shame, and I couldn't move on before I let those feelings go. That took work, and it also took therapy. It was thanks to an online group coaching session that I was able to learn the tools to help me unpick my toxic relationship with success. In our session, a woman was talking openly about her anxiety. The coach asked questions about the anxiety, what its job was, and why it was there. The woman realized that her anxiety showed up because she cared about the world, her loved ones, the future. It was her brain doing its best to get her through a confusing world. The coach then asked her to do something I didn't expect: *say thank you to these parts of yourselves*. The woman was saying thank you to the anxious parts of her mind for the first time. She was appreciating all aspects of herself, instead of scolding the anxiety for always ruining things. She started to see it as separate to her: she was not the anxiety. The anxiety wasn't *her*. Once we start leaning into all the feelings we find difficult, rather than pushing them away, their power over us lessens. That old phrase, 'What we resist, persists', still rings true. This is just one example of realizing that underneath our need for success, many of us also have some healing to do.

I had a breakthrough moment after befriending the parts of me that were success-obsessed. The side of me that felt competitive. The 'me' who was hustling and addicted to trying to be 'the best'. I realized these aspects of myself were products of our culture, products of a world telling us we have to be the best, otherwise we are lazy. I'd internalized this message, from school, from teachers; I never felt good enough. I was just trying my best in the only way I knew how. I found that once I befriended these parts of me, I was able to slowly let the shame go, and that's when true success started to blossom. You don't have to regret, or live with your past mistakes or failures hanging over you. This is one way to validate yourself, on your own terms.

Validation is a huge theme that came up again and again when I was discussing success with friends, colleagues and interviewees for this book. We are social animals: we want people to accept, validate and reassure us that we are doing the right things and going in the right direction. But this means that in order to receive validation from others, we can often do the wrong thing for ourselves. It takes courage to follow your own definition, your own path, to say 'no', to turn down things that culturally look successful on paper. Remembering that they can make us feel overwhelmed, trapped and out of alignment can help us to break free. Our bodies are intelligent, listen closely: that pang in your chest, that low ache in your stomach, that's telling you something. So are those moments when you smile, feel open-hearted and free. Trust your instincts.

Outward markers of success are shiny, and exciting and tempting; they make people sit up and notice; they can temporarily make you feel secure, valid and that you have the world's approval. They give you social rewards (money, access, ease). These are all things that are nice to have, for sure. It's reassuring and can impact our levels of comfort.

But the feelings of fulfilment and contentment usually come from all the other things we've discussed in this book – they come from being aware of the myths.

How much is your current version of success costing you? If it's costing you too much, what, if anything, are you prepared to give up? If you want more time to yourself, are you willing to say no more often, at the expense of your acquaintances' validation? If you want a less stressful life, does it mean changing jobs, even if your LinkedIn profile won't look so impressive? I think about this quote from Elizabeth Gilbert all the time: 'What are you willing to give up to have the life you keep pretending you want?' If you are not happy deep down, it's time to stop covering things up with more markers of success. It's likely there's less standing between you and that life than you think, you just need to get out of your own way and find another way to recognize your self-worth.

Something I've found useful is to make a list or a mood board of all the people I admire most in the world, be they friends or public figures. You can work out what your values are by acknowledging what you most respect in other people. For me it was:

- Integrity (not abandoning my gut feelings).
- Connection (finding a way to connect, not broadcast).

- Learning (being a forever student).
- Transparency (being open and honest about my feelings).
- Respect (respecting myself, my own boundaries and others').

Knowing our values can guide us to our true version of success, as when we're faced with a decision, we're more likely to make the right one for us, rather than follow the crowd. It can also encourage us to set stronger boundaries to ensure that we're living our daily lives in alignment with what we care about. A way to get to the root of your values is to remember *we aren't chasing success, we are chasing a feeling.* Money is safety. Ambition is feeling like your life is propelling forwards. Friendship makes us feel connected. Underneath all those things, we are wanting to feel a certain level of status, comfort or acceptance. There is nothing wrong with that, but once you start to acknowledge which feelings you are chasing, you can find a route to them in easier and more authentic ways.

Small Scale, Great Success

Through the course of writing this book, I have kept a list of the many different definitions of success that people shared with me during interviews I've done. Although they were individual and specific, whenever I looked at the list, I noticed five general themes arose with each one. (Remember, at the start of the book, 'success' was about things like getting a degree, buying a house, getting a good job, getting married, having kids, etc.).

The five themes and values that arose out of people's versions of success were as follows: time, love, peace, connection and hope. They just manifested themselves in different ways:

- **Warm relationships** – people felt happiest and most successful when they were with people, even one person, who understood them. It is that moment when you feel the **love** from someone in your life, whether that is a best friend, or a less 'traditional' friend in your life – the warmth of a connection with a stranger, a therapist, a teacher, a work colleague, or an acquaintance you meet up with a few times a year can be so impactful. Meaningful moments including feeling heard, feeling helpful to others and spending reciprocal time with people who are important to us give us that feeling of **connection**.

- **Having 'just enough'** – those moments of things being OK: a moment outside, a walk, a cup of tea in the garden, a house that feels like a home. Many people I spoke to said it felt like **peace**.

- **Radical self-acceptance** – moments when you accept that this is who you are. Accepting that is your life. Cultivating **love** for yourself and **connection** with who you truly are, including self-forgiveness. People said that being able to accept and forgive felt like success.
- **Carrying on**. That inner drive to want to keep moving forwards, despite things going wrong. Feelings of growing, striving, being challenged – moving towards a feeling of **hope**.
- Enough **money** – when people spoke about money, they didn't mention objects, they mentioned wanting freedom. Enough for themselves and their families. Safety. **Peace**.

The seemingly small things in between the milestones cropped up a lot during the interviews too – the cups of tea in bed, the sunrises and sunsets, a child stepping in a puddle, hearing the sounds of birds, long walks in nature, a text from a friend – i.e. having the time and space to even notice these small moments in life. This was usually connected to having a job and lifestyle that make room for living in the moment more too.

You can make a start without needing to think too far into the future, or thinking about the really huge life goals, but instead by working out what makes you happy now, on the smallest scale possible. How do we enjoy spending our minutes, hours, days? What seemingly insignificant mundane things make us feel slightly happier? How can we do more of those?

Success isn't looking up to a few famous, powerful people and thinking they have the answers. We all have the answers within us.

Here's the thing: when we are envious of successful people, we are actually just jealous because they have found *their* version of success.

The more I think about it, having covered various big topics in this book, the more I believe the biggest signs of success in life are liking yourself, rooting for yourself and backing yourself. Stripping away the external baggage weighing us down and realizing we are enough as we are. As the famous phrase attributed to Chinese philosopher Lao Tzu goes, 'To attain knowledge, add things every day. To attain wisdom, remove things every day.' Success is about not abandoning yourself. It's rediscovering that inner child inside all of us and leaning into the wisdom they are trying to share. We need to follow our gut instincts. We look outwards for so much, when we have the resources inside us to get through anything.

Final Chapter Reflections

1. **What *hasn't* been working so far?** Write a list of things that don't feel right, things that could look 'good' to the outside world but have never made you happy. By exploring the things that don't light you up, or things that don't work for you, you are moving forwards along a path towards the right place. Be honest.

2. **What are your values in life?** Can you pinpoint your intrinsic values and write them down on a piece of paper as a reminder when you need it? Do the words 'time', 'love', 'peace', 'connection' and 'hope' resonate with you?

3. **Instead of a 'to-do' list, write down a 'have-done' list.** Look at all the things you've done so far. Have a moment to take it all in before you embark on your next phase. What have you learned from observing what you've already done?

4. What is the *feeling* you want to arrive at, one day? What would arriving feel like when you got there? Explore that feeling, of finally arriving at the door of your dream life and think about ways you could allow yourself to experience that sensation now.

5. Write down your definition of personal success and check in on it regularly. Our definition of success is always changing and evolving and could change from one month to the next. Update accordingly, check in with yourself often.

Afterword

When our lives fall apart and things well and truly hit the fan, it's the normal, mundane moments we crave, not the dizzying heights of so-called success. When we lose someone, we crave the normality of sitting on the sofa with them. When we lose the job we love, we crave the small things like saying hello or making a cup of tea for colleagues. When we get ill, we crave enough energy to go for a short walk. When a global pandemic hits, we crave everyday activities like going to the cinema, or a dinner with a friend. But in our current success-obsessed society, the mundane moments mean nothing. They aren't celebrated in the media or at awards ceremonies. We reduce them down to being ridiculous and unimportant. We gloss over them, scrambling for the next thing. The next big hit. Ironically, it's these small moments of success that we cast aside, when really these are the moments that are in fact everything.

Writer Anne Lamott spoke beautifully about how we should

celebrate the 'ordinary life' more on Sam Fragoso's show *Talk Easy*: 'Hooray for ordinary lives, because that's where the nourishment is. It's not in some fantasy of what will happen once you're famous enough, or you've found the right person to marry or you make enough money or you get a new car. It's in the savouring and fully living the ordinary life that you're gonna find both the salvation and nourishment.' There is something inherently calming and freeing about not *just living* an 'ordinary' life (whether that's sometimes or all the time) but finding ways to savour each moment of it too. You can set all the intentions and grand plans you want for your future, but the fact is our lives have to be lived in the here and now.

This doesn't mean aiming high isn't worth it. It is. Life *is* about the forward motions, the excitement, the hope, the dreams and the growth. Have big dreams. Just make sure they are yours. And don't forget to just *be*, too.

I still have big things I want to do with my life, but I will not lose my perspective. I will not lose myself again in my quest for success. The pot of gold at the end of the rainbow may not exist, but it doesn't mean you can't enjoy the rainbow itself. I promise to enjoy the rainbow now. All of it.

Enjoy the ride, enjoy your success, whatever that means for *you*.

You deserve to be happy, and to see your life as a success. You have already arrived.

References

One

29 **'Do you know the *Ultimate Success Formula?*':** https://
www.facebook.com/TonyRobbins/photos/do-you-know-
the-ultimate-success-formula-learn-the-four-step-process-
and-start-t/10154518030209060/

34 **It's worth mentioning Gurley Brown didn't even like
the phrase 'Having It All':** https://www.nytimes.
com/2015/01/04/magazine/the-complicated-origins-of-
having-it-all.html

35 **'I felt the need to speak out once more':** https://www.
elizabethgilbert.com/against-balance-dear-ones-the-other-
night-at-my-event-in-st-paul-a-young/

37 **'For the first six months of my son's life':** https://www.
newstatesman.com/society/2022/06/childcare-flexibility-
working-mothers-stay-at-home

41 **'men in this century':** https://www.elizabethlesser.org/
keynote-speech-at-omega-institutes-2014-women-power-
conferencewomenmen-the-next-conversation

45 **'I understand we all have different backgrounds':** https://
podcasts.apple.com/gb/podcast/e110-molly-mae-how-she-
became-creative-director-of-plt-at-22/id1291423644?i=
1000544772150

46 **'I have the best advice for women in business':** https://
variety.com/2022/tv/features/kardashians-hulu-kris-kim-
khloe-1235198939/

47 **'What does it take to make it in modern Britain?':**
https://profilebooks.com/work/people-like-us/

51 **you were more likely to be successful if you were taller:**
https://www.bmj.com/content/352/bmj.i582

51 **easy to pronounce and common names:** https://online
library.wiley.com/doi/abs/10.1111/j.1468-0084.2011.00664.x

52 **'It is easier for more white people':** https://katemckean.
substack.com/p/how-do-you-define-success

53 **'Why success in life is the art of the possible':** https://
www.thetimes.co.uk/article/why-success-in-life-is-the-art-
of-the-possible-tj663nkjh

55 **'Dysgradia, a syndrome where there is a complete lack
of connection':** https://www.psychologytoday.com/us/
articles/199505/the-other-side-fame

57   **Damien Chazelle was only thirty-two when he won Best Director:** https://www.theguardian.com/film/2017/feb/27/damien-chazelle-wins-best-director-oscar-la-la-land-academy-awards-2017

57   **Zadie Smith wrote** *White Teeth* **aged twenty-one:** https://www.theguardian.com/books/2000/dec/11/fiction.whitbreadbookawards2000

59   **'Forbes 30 Under 30 is an awkward ego-fest':** https://erikhoel.substack.com/p/forbes-30-under-30-is-an-awkward

61   **'A contrarian isn't one who always objects':** https://medium.com/@RationalBadger/being-a-contrarian-757ab7c19d15

62   **'Very often audacity – not talent – makes one person an artist and another person a shadow artist':** Julia Cameron, *The Artist's Way: 25th Anniversary Edition*, Penguin, 2002

64   **'You become 42 per cent more likely to achieve your goals and dreams':** https://www.dominican.edu/sites/default/files/2020-02/gailmatthews-harvard-goals-researchsummary.pdf

65   **taken more risks in the workplace:** https://smallbusiness.co.uk/conflicted-brits-scared-take-risks-2542749/

Two

77   'melancholia', rather than happiness: https://www.idler.co.uk/article/a-brief-history-of-melancholy/

77   one in seven people in England now takes an antidepressant: https://www.thetimes.co.uk/article/antidepressant-use-in-england-rises-by-a-fifth-rsfzrfmwm

78   'so stressed at some point over the last year': https://www.mentalhealth.org.uk/about-us/news/survey-stressed-nation-UK-overwhelmed-unable-to-cope

78   'persistent feelings of sadness or hopelessness': https://www.cdc.gov/media/releases/2022/p0331-youth-mental-health-covid-19.html

78   60 per cent of all UK workers are unhappy at work: https://www.hrmagazine.co.uk/content/news/60-of-uk-workers-unhappy-in-their-jobs

83   so-called negative emotions could be key to our wellbeing: https://www.scientificamerican.com/article/negative-emotions-key-well-being/#:~:text=Negative%20emotions%20also%20most%20likely,suppressing%20them%20is%20so%20fruitless

88   'it's only once we combine our emotions or anxieties': https://www.hodder.co.uk/titles/jill-bolte-taylor/my-stroke-of-insight/9780340980507/

Three

99   **'Listening to a podcast':** https://twitter.com/sianharries_/status/1458066958386073606

104   **'The 1980s were, "Put on a suit and work till you drop",':** https://www.theguardian.com/money/2021/apr/22/burnt-out-is-the-exhausting-cult-of-productivity-finally-over

107   **'For people in high-stress jobs':** https://www.sleepfoundation.org/sleep-hygiene/revenge-bedtime-procrastination

110   **'In my old life every ticking minute was accounted for':** https://www.thetimes.co.uk/article/at-32-my-burnout-hit-me-hard-8rfzbprwm

117   **using a Pomodoro timer:** https://pomofocus.io/

117   **something I learned from therapist Anna Mathur:** https://podcasts.apple.com/gb/podcast/the-therapy-edit/id1505968557

117   **'Sometimes a little chaos gets things done':** https://longform.org/posts/how-taffy-brodesser-akner-thrives-on-stress#:~:text=Everyone%20wants%20women%20to%20be,little%20chaos%20gets%20things%20done

120   **90 per cent of employees admit they have gone to work when sick:** https://press.roberthalf.com/2019-10-24-9-In-10-Employees-Come-To-Work-Sick-Survey-Shows

123   **'Rest is like breathing or running':** https://psyche.co/
guides/how-to-rest-well-and-enjoy-a-more-creative-
sustainable-life

124   **there are many different types of rest:** https://www.
samanthaand.co/

126   **'spoon theory,' coined by Christine Miserandino:**
https://butyoudontlooksick.com/articles/written-by-
christine/the-spoon-theory/

126   **Author Simon Sinek uses the analogy of 'coins':** https://
simonsinek.com

127   **'productivity dysmorphia':** https://www.
annacodrearado.com/podcast

Four

140   **'Influencers, entrepreneurs, people whose bedrooms
are also their office':** https://www.theguardian.com/
lifeandstyle/2022/jan/23/if-influencers-dont-believe-in-
fairytale-endings-then-who-wil-molly-mae-hague

142   **'objectification in the workplace':** https://www.
frontiersin.org/articles/10.3389/fpsyg.2021.651071/full

143   **'[. . .] when you do something and it's successful':**
https://www.irishexaminer.com/lifestyle/artsandculture/
arid-40068521.html

143 **Sometimes it is how we label ourselves:** https://
arthurbrooks.com/article/you-are-not-your-work/

145 **'a diagnosis often given to women':** https://hbr.org/
2021/02/stop-telling-women-they-have-imposter-
syndrome

146 **'Yes, you're an impostor':** https://seths.blog/2017/10/
imposter-syndrome/

149 **'Working is not everything about who I am':** https://
www.youtube.com/watch?v=3L4m5ZMzf3A

Five

155 **'I was curled up, uncontrollably crying':** https://
podcasts.apple.com/gb/podcast/e182-alex-scott-ive-
never-told-the-full-truth-about-my-past/id1291423644?i=
1000580993241

156 **'renowned during one's lifetime':** https://magazine.
columbia.edu/article/long-and-strange-history-celebrity

159 **'Baby boomers made up the first consumer generation':**
https://www.theatlantic.com/sponsored/raymond-
james/when-boomers-rule-the-world-again/262/

161 **'20 million calls, with 7.4 million for the final':** https://
www.theguardian.com/media/2009/aug/26/big-brother-
in-figures

163 **'toxic', 'a disease':** Joey Berlin, *Toxic Fame: Celebrities Speak on Stardom,* (Visible Ink Press, 1996)

163 **'the average life span of a celebrity is only 58 years':** Ibid.

166 **'birds skimming the water':** Emma Nicolson, Busy Being Free: A Lifelong Romantic is Seduced by Solitude, (Weidenfeld & Nicolson, 2022)

167 **'the iron cage':** https://www.thoughtco.com/understanding-max-webers-iron-cage-3026373

169 **'the Oscars takes place in a shopping centre':** https://twitter.com/LindseyKelk/status/1508182679300173824

169 **'the age of boring celebrity':** https://www.newstatesman.com/culture/2022/05/a-mundane-met-gala-shows-we-are-in-the-age-of-boring-celebrity

169 **78 per cent of Gen Z teens would be willing to share personally identifiable data:** https://www.pewresearch.org/wp-content/uploads/sites/3/2010/10/millennials-confident-connected-open-to-change.pdf

170 **70 per cent of teenage subscribers said they can relate more to YouTubers:** https://www.thinkwithgoogle.com/marketing-strategies/video/youtube-stars-influence/

170 **'32% of Gen Zers and 28% of Millennials':** https://www.pewresearch.org/science/2021/05/26/gen-z-millennials-stand-out-for-climate-change-activism-social-media-engagement-with-issue/

171 **A 2019 study by Lego:** https://theharrispoll.com/briefs/
lego-group-kicks-off-global-program-to-inspire-the-next-
generation-of-space-explorers-as-nasa-celebrates-50-years-
of-moon-landing/

172 **'It really doesn't take much to be a celebrity now':**
Berlin, *Toxic Fame*

174 **'I've also spent hours watching perfect girls online':**
https://www.standard.co.uk/lifestyle/london-life/
instagram-star-essena-o-neill-quits-unhealthy-social-media-
claiming-it-has-created-a-brainwashed-generation-a3105621.
html

174 **'And why the fuck am I so unfucking unhappy'?:**
https://www.youtube.com/watch?v=WKKwgq9LRgA

176 **'There's infrastructure power':** https://www.thejournal.
ie/caitlin-moran-interview-4221002-Sep2018/

Six

181 **'becoming financially stable':** https://twitter.com/
Chelsea_Fagan/status/1549095377290371081?t=fVqIOKgns
QbA6vYs828AbA&s=03

181 **'a 24-hour rotating display of materialism and disparity':**
https://www.cnet.com/culture/showing-off-wealth-on-
social-media-get-ready-for-the-backlash/

181   **a 2018 study published by Sage Journals:** www-personal.
umich.edu/~smgarcia/pubs/Status_Signals_Paradox.pdf

183   **the current average salary in the UK is £27,756:** https://
standout-cv.com/pages/average-uk-salary

186   **'obsessive, envious, keeping-up-with-the-Joneses':**
https://www.penguin.co.uk/books/343470/
affluenza-by-james-oliver/9780091900113

193   **'Over time the long-term growth rates of happiness':**
https://www.iza.org/publications/dp/13923/the-easterlin-
paradox%2523:~:text=The%252520Easterlin%252520
Paradox%252520states%252520that,the%252520contradict
ion%252520is%252520social%252520comparison

193   **the offspring of very affluent parents:** https://www.
psychologytoday.com/gb/articles/201311/the-problem-
rich-kids#:~:text=In%20a%20surprising%20switch%
2C%20the,meaning%20to%20having%20it%20all

194   **'Unsustainable consumption':** https://timesofindia.
indiatimes.com/city/delhi/our-greed-has-a-bearing-on-
pollution-climate-change/articleshow/73629726.cms

195   **boohoo, has come under scrutiny for allegedly paying
its factory workers as little as £3.50 an hour:** https://
www.thetimes.co.uk/article/boohoo-fashion-giant-faces-
slavery-investigation-57s3hxcth#:~:text=Workers%20
in%20Leicester%20making%20clothes,Sunday%20
Times%20investigation%20has%20found

195 **'a figure within our mythology':** https://www.youtube.
com/watch?v=WJoD4O4PA5M

Seven

207 **'After a lifetime of saying "yes"':** https://www.thecut.
com/2017/09/what-happens-to-ambition-in-your-30s.html

207 **'Where does ambition go':** https://gen.medium.com/
where-did-my-ambition-go-c800ab4ad01d

208 **a cohort of 'exhausted, type-A millennial workers':**
https://www.nytimes.com/2021/04/21/technology/
welcome-to-the-yolo-economy.html

215 **'the reality often fell short of that dream':** https://www.
elle.com/uk/life-and-culture/elle-voices/a40652210/
beyond-girlboss-next/

216 **our drive and ambition peaks at the age of thirty-three:**
https://www.independent.co.uk/life-style/bupa-study-
drive-ambition-age-33-a9307871.html

218 **global venture-capital funding for female founders:**
https://news.crunchbase.com/venture/global-vc-funding-
to-female-founders/

218 **It's even less for Black women:** https://news.crunchbase.
com/diversity/something-ventured-black-women-founders/

218 **'54,000 women a year':** https://pregnantthenscrewed.
com/about-maternity-discrimination/

218 **99.19 per cent of the technicians, mechanics and electricians:** https://careersmart.org.uk/occupations/equality/which-jobs-do-men-and-women-do-occupational-breakdown-gender

219 **'It's as if the women have cleared spaces in their lives':** https://medium.com/the-cut/the-ambition-collision-bb95136ccea3

223 **'All that chatter about minutes and seconds':** Sarah Moss, *Summerwater* (Picador, 2020)

223 **'Gardening was mine and mine alone':** https://farrah.substack.com/p/the-importance-of-being-mediocre

233 **'Upper limiting', coined by author Gay Hendricks:** https://www.goodreads.com/book/show/6391876-the-big-leap

237 **'Economic growth accompanied by worsening social outcomes':** https://www.globalcitizen.org/en/content/jacinda-ardern-goalkeepers-unga-2019/

238 **'So what if I was on calls seven days a week':** https://www.youtube.com/watch?v=rtsHUeKnkC8

Eight

244 **'The reason we're so obsessed with social media':** https://podcasts.apple.com/gb/podcast/how-to-seek-joy-with-martha-beck/id1448401154?i=1000519269162

246   **'People can view this limbo state as negative':** https://
www.elle.com/uk/life-and-culture/a36716159/
inbetweener-life-uncertainty/

250   **'what is impressive and glitzy can be fabricated':** Jamie
Varon, *Radically Content: Being Satisfied in an Endlessly
Dissatisfied World* (Rock Point, 2022)

257   **'But it was only five people, six, and 13':** https:// www.
theguardian.com/global/2019/sep/08/gillian-anderson-i-
fall-in-love-with-my-characters

259   **'There's a lot of importance placed on the "work" of
maintaining romantic relationships':** https://twitter.
com/Chelsea_Fagan/status/1507334863682248708

260   **'Who are these actual adults':** https://twitter.com/
jamieklingler/status/1497190041994333931

260   **there is often a 'premium placed on romantic love
culturally.':** https://thepanoptic.co.uk/2018/04/30/
everything-i-know-about-love/

262   **'I've had three marriages with the same husband.':**
https://www.cbc.ca/player/play/1443274307913

264   **my debut novel *OLIVE*:** https://uk.bookshop.org/books/
olive-9780008382728/9780008382735

265   **I wrote about it for *ELLE*:** https://www.elle.com/uk/
life-and-culture/culture/a33009251/motherhood-rejection/

265   **I wrote about it for [. . .] *Grazia*:** https://graziadaily.co.uk/
life/real-life/emma-gannon-olive-childfree-by-choice/

265 **I wrote about it for [. . .]** *Marie Claire*: https://www.marieclaire.co.uk/life/sex-and-relationships/emma-gannon-childfree-by-choice-women-704727

267 **In his** *The School of Life* **video called 'To Have or Not to Have Children'**: www.youtube.com/watch?v=f8RPUJhULLE

268 **Jennifer Albright tweeted: 'I was gonna put a downpayment on a house'**: https://twitter.com/Bowsnonk/status/864178329657655296?ref_src=twsrc%5Etfw%7Ctwcamp%5Etweetembed%7Ctwterm%5E8641783 29657655296%7Ctwgr%5E0203f613f0289678f4cfa0899cc83425 7719e76b%7Ctwcon%5Es1_&ref_url=https%3A%2F%2Fwww.buzzfeed.com%2Fbradesposito%2Famerica-has-discovered-the-anti-avocado-toast-millionaire

269 **'For anyone who needs to hear it'**: https://twitter.com/pollyosborn/status/1490693436974026755

Nine

273 **'I'm not willing to spend my life racing to the top of the mountain'**: https://www.instagram.com/p/Cl9PZ6AoNXB/?hl=en

275 **the 'illusion that once we make it'**: https://www.nytimes.com/2019/05/28/smarter-living/you-accomplished-something-great-so-now-what.html#:~:

text=%E2%80%9CArrival%20fallacy%20is%20this%20illusion,credited%20with%20coining%20the%20term

277   **'Success is a temporary thrill':** https://twitter.com/AdamMGrant/status/1518244137082011648?lang=en

280   **'Can't I just cut to the good part?':** https://misshezah.substack.com/p/im-not-a-checklist-person-but-

285   **'When I think about success':** https://thehyphen.substack.com/p/the-meaning-of-success-has-drastically/comments

294   **'What are you willing to give up':** https://cokecmosummit.com/2018/11/big-magic-creative-living-beyond-fear-with-elizabeth-gilbert/

Afterword

302   **'Hooray for ordinary lives':** https://podcasts.apple.com/us/podcast/sunday-school-with-author-anne-lamott/id1100417601?i=1000514712754

Acknowledgements

Thank you to:

My past self, I'm sorry for being so hard on you.

My current self, I'm glad I slowed down to be with you.

My wise inner self, thank you for guiding me forwards.

Jo Gannon, for always being there.

Paul Storrie, for loving every version of me.

My friends, for being a safe island every time I need a break from the waves.

Charlotte Clarke, for knowing me so well.

Viola Hayden, for your enthusiasm, encouragement and friendship.

Lucy Oates, for your smart brain and sharp editorial eye.

Becky Short, Izzie Ghaffari-Parker and Sophie Bruce for your energy and ideas.

Helena Gonda, for believing in this book from the very beginning.

Abigail Bergstrom, for the voice notes and kitchen table chats.

Kim Butler, for everything we achieved together.

Natalie Lue, for teaching me how to say no.

Selina Barker, for encouraging me to dream big while also taking care of myself.

Julia Cameron, for giving me the tools to always find the way back home to myself.

Permissions

Emma Gannon is a *Sunday Times* bestselling author, broadcaster, coach, speaker, novelist and creator of the number one multi-million-downloaded careers podcast in the UK, *Ctrl Alt Delete*. She has been a columnist for *The Times*, the *Telegraph* and *Courier* magazine.

Emma has published five bestselling books to date, including *The Multi-Hyphen Method, Sabotage, Disconnected* and her debut novel, *OLIVE*, which was nominated for the Dublin Literary Award in 2022.

Emma writes a popular weekly newsletter called *The Hyphen* that is an exploration of ideas that have got her thinking in new ways. She is proud to be an ambassador for The Prince's Trust and the World Literacy Foundation.